ADVANCED FOOD CHEMISTRY

ADVANCED FOOD CHEMISTRY

By

Dr. Syed Aftab Iqbal
M.Sc., Ph.D., FICS
FICC, FIAEM, MNASc.
Professor
Department of Chemistry
Saifia Science College
Barkatullah University
Bhopal (India)

&

Ms. Neelofar Iqbal
B.Ed., M.Sc.
Executive Editor
Oriental Journal of
Computer Science & Technnology
(India)

DPH

DISCOVERY PUBLISHING HOUSE PVT. LTD.
NEW DELHI-110 002

Published by:
Tilak Wasan
DISCOVERY PUBLISHING HOUSE PVT. LTD.
4383/4B, Ansari Road, Darya Ganj
New Delhi-110 002 (India)
Phone : +91-11-23279245, 43596065, 23253475
E-mail : discoverybooksindia@gmail.com
discoverypublishinghouse@gmail.com
namitwasan9@gmail.com
web : www.discoverypublishinggroup.com

***First Edition:* 2011**

ISBN: 978-81-8356-749-7

Advanced Food Chemistry

Printed at:
Infinity Imaging Systems
Delhi

Preface

Food chemistry is the study of chemical processes and interactions of all biological and non-biological components of foods. The biological substances include such items as meat, poultry, lettuce, beer, and milk as examples. It is similar to biochemistry in its main components such as carbohydrates, lipids, and protein, but it also includes areas such as water, vitamins, minerals, enzymes, food additives, flavours, and colours. This discipline also encompasses how products change under certain food processing techniques and ways either to enhance or to prevent them from happening. An example of enhancing a process would be to encourage fermentation of dairy products with microorganisms that convert lactose to lactic acid; an example of preventing a process would be stopping the browning on the surface of freshly cut Red Delicious apples using lemon juice or other acidulated water.

Food chemistry's history dates back as far as the late 1700s when many famous chemists were involved in discovering chemicals important in foods, including Carl Wilhelm Scheele (isolated malic acid from apples in 1785), and Sir Humphry Davy (published the first ever book on agricultural and food chemistry in 1813 titled Elements of

Agricultural Chemistry, in a Course of Lectures for the Board of Agriculture in the United Kingdom which would serve as a foundation for the profession worldwide, going into a fifth edition.

It was also out of concern for the quality of the food supply, mainly food adulteration and contamination issues that would first stem from intentional contamination to later with chemical food additives by the 1950s. The development of colleges and universities worldwide, most notably in the United States, would expand food chemistry as well with research of the dietary substances, most notably the Single-grain experiment during 1907-11. Additional research by Harvey W. Wiley at the United States Department of Agriculture during the late 19th century would play a key factor in the creation of the United States Food and Drug Administration in 1906. The American Chemical Society would establish their Agricultural and Food Chemistry Division in 1908 while the Institute of Food Technologists would establish their Food Chemistry Division in 1995.

Food science is a discipline concerned with all technical aspects of food, beginning with harvesting or slaughtering, and ending with its cooking and consumption. It is considered one of the agricultural sciences, and is usually considered distinct from the field of nutrition.

Author

Contents

CHAPTER

1

Introduction

FOOD CHEMISTRY

Food chemistry is the study of chemical processes and interactions of all biological and non-biological components of foods. The biological substances include such items as meat, poultry, lettuce, beer, and milk as examples. It is similar to biochemistry in its main components such as carbohydrates, lipids, and protein, but it also includes areas such as water, vitamins, minerals, enzymes, food additives, flavours, and colours. This discipline also encompasses how products change under certain food processing techniques and ways either to enhance or to prevent them from happening. An example of enhancing a process would be to encourage fermentation of dairy products with microorganisms that convert lactose to lactic acid; an example of preventing a process would be stopping the browning on the surface of freshly cut Red Delicious apples using lemon juice or other acidulated water.

History of Food Chemistry

Food chemistry's history dates back as far as the late 1700s when many famous chemists were involved in discovering chemicals important in foods, including Carl Wilhelm Scheele (isolated malic acid from apples in 1785), and Sir Humphry Davy (published the first ever book on agricultural and food chemistry in 1813 titled Elements of Agricultural Chemistry, in a Course of Lectures for the Board of Agriculture in the United Kingdom which would serve as a foundation for the profession worldwide, going into a fifth edition.

In 1874 the Society of Public Analysts was formed, with the aim of applying analytical methods to the benefit of the public It's early experiments were based on bread, milk and wine.

It was also out of concern for the quality of the food supply, mainly food adulteration and contamination issues that would first stem from intentional contamination to later with chemical food additives by the 1950s. The development of colleges and universities worldwide, most notably in the United States, would expand food chemistry as well with research of the dietary substances, most notably the Single-grain experiment during 1907-11. Additional research by Harvey W. Wiley at the United States Department of Agriculture during the late 19th century would play a key factor in the creation of the United States Food and Drug Administration in 1906. The American Chemical Society would establish their Agricultural and Food Chemistry Division in 1908 while the Institute of Food Technologists would establish their Food Chemistry Division in 1995.

Water

A major component of food is water, which can encompass anywhere from 50% in meat products to 95% in lettuce, cabbage, and tomato products. It is also an excellent place for bacterial growth and food spoilage if it is not properly processed. One way this is measured in food is by water activity which is very important in the shelf life of many foods during processing. One of the keys to food preservation in most instances is reduce the amount of water or alter the water's characteristics to enhance shelf-life. Such methods include dehydration, freezing, and refrigeration.

Carbohydrates

Comprising 75% of the biological world and 80% of all food intake for human consumption, the most common known human carbohydrate is starch. The simplest version of a carbohydrate is a monosaccharide which possesses the properties of carbon, hydrogen, and oxygen in a 1:2:1 ratio under a general formula of CnH_2nOn where n is a minimum of 3. Glucose is an example of a monosaccharide as is fructose. Combine them in the picture shown to the right and you have sucrose, one of the more common sugar products around. A chain of monosaccharides form to make a polysaccharide. Such polysaccharides include pectin, dextran, agar, and xanthan.

Sugar content is commonly measured in degrees brix.

Lipids

The term lipid comprises a diverse range of molecules and to some extent is a catchall for relatively water-insoluble or nonpolar compounds of biological origin, including waxes, fatty acids (including essential fatty acids), fatty-acid derived phospholipids, sphingolipids, glycolipids and terpenoids, such as retinoids and steroids. Some lipids are linear aliphatic molecules, while others have ring structures. Some are aromatic, while others are not. Some are flexible, while others are rigid.

Most lipids have some polar character in addition to being largely nonpolar. Generally, the bulk of their structure is nonpolar or hydrophobic ("water-fearing"), meaning that it does not interact well with polar solvents like water. Another part of their structure is polar or hydrophilic ("water-loving") and will tend to associate with polar solvents like water. This makes them amphiphilic molecules (having both hydrophobic and hydrophilic portions). In the case of cholesterol, the polar group is a mere -OH (hydroxyl or alcohol).

Lipids in food include the oils of such grains as corn, soybean, from animal fats, and are parts of many foods such as milk, cheese, and meat. They also act as vitamin carriers as well.

Proteins

Proteins compose over 50% of the dry weight of an average living cell and are very complex macromolecules. They also play a fundamental role in the structure and function of cells. Comprised mainly of carbon, hydrogen, oxygen, and some sulfur, they also may contain iron, copper, phosphorus, or zinc.

In food, proteins are essential for growth and survival and vary depending upon a person's age and physiology (e.g., pregnancy). Proteins in food are commonly found in peanuts, meat, poultry, and seafood. They are also involved in ELISA test for food allergy determination as well.

Enzymes

Enzymes are biochemical catalysts used in converting processes from one substance to another. They are also involved in reducing the amount of time and energy required to complete a chemical process. Many aspects of the food industry use catalysts, including baking, brewing, dairy, and fruit juices, to make cheese, beer, and bread.

Vitamins

Vitamins are nutrients required in small amounts for essential metabolic reactions in the body. These are broken down in nutrition as either water soluble (Vitamin C) or fat soluble (Vitamin E). An adequate supply of vitamins can prevent such diseases as beriberi, anemia, and scurvy while an overdose of vitamins can produce nausea and vomiting or even death.

Minerals

Dietary minerals in foods are large and diverse with many required to function while other trace elements can be hazardous if consumed in excessive amounts. Bulk minerals with a Reference Daily Intake (RDI, formerly Recommended Daily Allowance (RDA)) of more than 200 mg/day are calcium, magnesium, and potassium while important trace minerals (RDI less than 200 mg/day) are copper, iron, and zinc. These are found in many foods, but can also be taken in dietary supplements.

Food Colouring

Food colouring is added to change the color of any food substance. It is mainly for sensory analysis purposes. It can be used to simulate the natural color of a product as perceived by the customer, such as red dye like FD & C Red No. 40 (Allura Red AC) to ketchup or to add unnatural colors to a product like Kellogg's Froot Loops. Caramel is a natural food dye; the industrial form, caramel coloring, is the most widely-used food coloring and is found in foods from soft drinks to soy sauce, bread, and pickles.

Flavours

Flavour in food is important in how food smells and tastes to the consumer, especially in sensory analysis. Some of these products occur naturally like salt and sugar, but flavour chemists (called a "flavourist") develop many of these flavors for food products. Such artificial flavors include methyl salicylate which creates the wintergreen odor and lactic acid which gives milk a tart taste.

Food Additives

Food additives are substances added to food for preserving flavors, or improving taste or appearance. These processes are as old as adding vinegar for pickling or as an emulsifier for emulsion mixtures like mayonnaise. These are generally listed by "E number" in the European Union or GRAS ("Generally recognized as safe") by the United States Food and Drug Administration.

FOOD TECHNOLOGY

Food technology, or Food tech for short is the application of food science to the selection, preservation, processing, packaging, distribution, and use of safe, nutritious, and wholesome food.

Food scientists and food technologists study the physical, microbiological, and chemical makeup of food. Depending on their area of specialization, food scientists may develop ways to process, preserve, package, or store food, according to industry and government specifications and regulations. Consumers seldom think of the vast array of foods and the research and development that has resulted in the means to deliver tasty, nutritious, safe, and convenient foods.

In some schools, food technology is part of the curriculum and teaches, alongside how to cook, nutrition and the food manufacturing process.

Early History of Food Technology

Research in the field now known as food technology has been conducted for decades. Nicolas Appert's development in 1810 of the canning process was a decisive event. The process wasn't called canning then and Appert did not really know the principle on which his process worked, but canning has had a major impact on food preservation techniques.

Louis Pasteur's research on the spoilage of wine and his description of how to avoid spoilage in 1864 was an early attempt to put food technology on a scientific basis. Besides research into wine spoilage, Pasteur did research on the production of alcohol, vinegar, wines and beer, and the souring of milk. He developed pasteurization—the process of heating milk and milk products to destroy food spoilage and disease-producing organisms. In his research into food technology, Pasteur became the pioneer into bacteriology and of modern preventive medicine.

By 1940s to 1950s, the original four departments that had taught the subject under different names (including those at the University of Massachusetts and the University of California) had been retitled "food science", "food science and technology", or a similar variant.

Developments in Food Technology

Several companies in the food industry have played a role in the development of food technology. These developments have contributed greatly to the food supply. Some of these developments are:

- **Instantized Milk Powder** - D.D. Peebles (U.S. patent 2,835,586) developed the first instant milk powder, which has become the basis for a variety of new products that are rehydratable in cold water or milk. This process increases the surface area of the powdered product by partially rehydrating spray-dried milk powder.
- **Freeze Drying** - The first application of freeze drying was most likely in the pharmaceutical industry; however, a successful large-scale industrial application of the process was the development of continuous freeze drying of coffee.
- **High-Temperature Short Time Processing** - These processes for the most part are characterized by rapid

heating and cooling, holding for a short time at a relatively high temperature and filling aseptically into sterile containers.

- **Decaffeination of Coffee and Tea** - Decaffeinated coffee and tea was first developed on a commercial basis in Europe around 1900. The process is described in U.S. patent 897,763. Green coffee beans are treated with steam or water to around 20% moisture. The added water and heat separate the caffeine from the bean to its surface. Solvents are then used to remove the caffeine from the beans. In the 1980s, new non-organic solvent techniques have been developed for the decaffeination of coffee and tea. Carbon dioxide under supercritical conditions is one of these new techniques. U.S. patent 4,820,537 was issued to General Foods Corp. for a CO_2 decaffeination process.
- **Process optimization-** Food Technology now allows production of foods to be more efficient, Oil saving technologies are now available on different forms. Production methods and methodology have also become increasingly sophisticated.

FOOD SCIENCE

Food science is a discipline concerned with all technical aspects of food, beginning with harvesting or slaughtering, and ending with its cooking and consumption. It is considered one of the agricultural sciences, and is usually considered distinct from the field of nutrition.

Examples

Examples of the activities of food scientists include the development of new food products, design of processes to produce these foods, choice of packaging materials, shelf-life studies, sensory evaluation of the product with trained expert panels or potential consumers, as well as microbiological and chemical testing. Food scientists at universities may study more fundamental phenomena that are directly linked to the production of particular food product and its properties. In the U.S., food science is typically studied at land-grant universities.

Food science is a highly interdisciplinary applied science. It incorporates concepts from many different fields including microbiology, chemical engineering, biochemistry, and many others.

Some of the subdisciplines of food science include:

- **Food safety** - the causes, prevention and communication dealing with foodborne illness.
- **Food microbiology** - the positive and negative interactions between micro-organisms and foods.
- **Food preservation** - the causes and prevention of quality degradation.
- **Food engineering** - the industrial processes used to manufacture food.
- **Product development** - the invention of new food products.
- **Sensory analysis** - the study of how food is perceived by the consumer's senses.
- **Food chemistry** - the molecular composition of food and the involvement of these molecules in chemical reactions.
- **Food packaging** - the study of how packaging is used to preserve food after it has been processed and contain it through distribution.
- **Molecular gastronomy** - the scientific investigation of processes in cooking, social and artistic gastronomical phenomena.
- **Food technology** - the technological aspects.
- **Food physics** - the physical aspects of foods (such as viscosity, creaminess, and texture).

The main organization in the United States regarding food science and food technology is the Institute of Food Technologists (IFT), headquartered in Chicago, Illinois, which is the US member organisation of the International Union of Food Science and Technology (IUFoST). The European national organisations are organised into the European Federation of Food Science and Technology (EFFoST), based at Wageningen University, the Netherlands.

Some popular books on some aspects of food science or kitchen science have been written by Harold McGee and Howard Hillman.

In the October 2006 issue of Food Technology, 2006-07 IFT President Dennis R. Heldman noted that the IFT Committee on Higher Education gave the current definition of food science as follows: "Food Science is the discipline in which the engineering, biological, and physical sciences are used to study the nature of foods, the causes of deterioration, the principles underlying food processing, and the improvement of foods for the consuming public."

CHAPTER

2

Food

Food is any substance, usually composed of carbohydrates, fats, proteins and water, that can be eaten or drunk by an animal or human for nutrition or pleasure. Items considered food may be sourced from plants, animals or other categories such as fungus or fermented products like alcohol. Although many human cultures sought food items through hunting and gathering, today most cultures use farming, ranching, and fishing, with hunting, foraging and other methods of a local nature included but playing a minor role.

Most traditions have a recognizable cuisine, a specific set of cooking traditions, preferences, and practices, the study of which is known as gastronomy. Many cultures have diversified their foods by means of preparation, cooking methods and manufacturing. This also includes a complex food trade which helps the cultures to economically survive by-way-of food, not just by consumption.

Many cultures study the dietary analysis of food habits. While humans are omnivores, religion and social constructs such as morality often affect which foods they will consume. Food safety is also a concern with foodborne illness claiming many lives each year. In many languages, food is often used metaphorically or figuratively, as in "food for thought".

FOOD SOURCES

Almost all foods are of plant or animal origin, although there are some exceptions. Foods not coming from animal or plant sources include various edible fungi, such as mushrooms. Fungi and ambient bacteria are used in the preparation of fermented and pickled foods such as leavened bread, alcoholic drinks, cheese, pickles, and yogurt. Many cultures eat seaweed, a protist, or blue-green algae (cyanobacteria) such as Spirulina. Additionally, salt is often eaten as a flavoring or preservative, and baking soda is used in food preparation. Both of these are inorganic substances, as is water, an important part of human diet. A variety of foods from plant sourcesMany plants or plant parts are eaten as food. There are around 2,000 plant species which are cultivated for food, and many have several distinct cultivars.

Seeds of plants are a good source of food for animals, including humans because they contain nutrients necessary for the plant's initial growth. In fact, the majority of food consumed by human beings are seed-based foods. Edible seeds include cereals (such as maize, wheat, and rice), legumes (such as beans, peas, and lentils), and nuts. Oilseeds are often pressed to produce rich oils, such as sunflower, rapeseed (including canola oil), and sesame.

One of the earliest food recipes made from ground chickpeas is called hummus, which can be traced back to Ancient Egypt times. Fruits are the ripened ovaries of plants, including the seeds within. Many plants have evolved fruits that are attractive as a food source to animals, so that animals will eat the fruits and excrete the seeds some distance away. Fruits, therefore, make up a significant part of the diets of most cultures. Some botanical fruits, such as tomatoes, pumpkins and eggplants, are eaten as vegetables.

Vegetables are a second type of plant matter that is commonly eaten as food. These include root vegetables (such as potatoes and carrots), leaf vegetables (such as spinach and lettuce), stem vegetables (such as bamboo shoots and asparagus), and inflorescence vegetables (such as globe artichokes and broccoli). Many herbs and spices are highly-flavorful vegetables.

Animals

Animals can be used as food either directly, or indirectly by the products they produce. Meat is an example of a direct product taken from an animal, which comes from either muscle systems or from organs. Food products produced by animals include milk produced by mammals, which in many cultures is drunk or processed into dairy products such as cheese or butter. In addition birds and other animals lay eggs, which are often eaten, and bees produce honey, a popular sweetener in many cultures. Some cultures consume blood, some in the form of blood sausage, as a thickener for sauces, a cured salted form for times of food scarcity, and others use blood in stews such as civet.

PRODUCTION

Food is traditionally obtained through farming, ranching, and fishing, with hunting, foraging and other methods of subsistence locally important. More recently, there has been a growing trend towards more sustainable agricultural practices. This approach, which is partly fueled by consumer demand, encourages biodiversity, local self-reliance and organic farming methods Major influences on food production are international organizations, (e.g. the World Trade Organization and Common Agricultural Policy), national government policy (or law), and war.

Preparation

While some food can be eaten raw, many foods undergo some form of preparation for reasons of safety, palatability, or flavor. At the simplest level this may involve washing, cutting, trimming or adding other foods or ingredients, such as spices. It may also involve mixing, heating or cooling, pressure cooking, fermentation, or combination with other food. In a home, most food preparation takes place in a kitchen. Some preparation is done to enhance the taste or aesthetic appeal; other preparation may help to preserve the food; and others may be involved in cultural identity. A meal is made up of food which is prepared to be eaten at a specific time and place.

Animal Preparation

The preparation of animal-based food will usually involve slaughter, evisceration, hanging, portioning and rendering. In developed countries, this is usually done outside the home in slaughterhouses which are used to process animals en mass for meat production. Many countries regulate their slaughterhouses by law. For example, the United States has established the Humane Slaughter Act of 1958, which requires that an animal be stunned before killing. This act, like those in many countries, exempts slaughter in accordance to religious law, such as kosher shechita and dhabiha halal. Strict interpretations of kashrut require the animal to be fully aware when its carotid artery is cut.

On the local level, a butcher may commonly break down larger animal meat into smaller manageable cuts and pre-wrapped for commercial sale or wrapped to order in butcher paper. In addition, fish and seafood may be fabricated into smaller cuts by a fish monger at the local level. However fish butchery may be done on board a fishing vessel and quick-frozen for preservation of quality.

Cooking

The term "cooking" encompasses a vast range of methods, tools and combinations of ingredients to improve the flavour or digestibility of food. Cooking technique, known as culinary art, generally requires the selection, measurement and combining of ingredients in an ordered procedure in an effort to achieve the desired result. Constraints on success include the variability of ingredients, ambient conditions, tools, and the skill of the individual cooking The diversity of cooking worldwide is a reflection of the myriad nutritional, aesthetic, agricultural, economic, cultural and religious considerations that impact upon it.

Cooking requires applying heat to a food which usually, though not always, chemically transforms it, thus changing its flavor, texture, appearance, and nutritional properties. Cooking proper, as opposed to roasting, requires the boiling of water in a container, and was practiced at least since the 10th millennium BC with the introduction of pottery There is archaeological evidence of roasted foodstuffs at Homo erectus campsites dating from 420,000 years ago.

Cooking Equipment and Methods

There are many types of cooking equipment used for cooking. Ovens are one type of cooking equipment which can be used for baking or roasting and offer a dry-heat cooking method. Different cuisines will use different types of ovens, for example Indian culture uses a Tandoor oven is a cylindrical clay oven which operates at a single high temperature while western kitchens will use variable temperature convection ovens, conventional ovens, toaster ovens in addition to non-radiant heat ovens like the microwave oven. Ovens may be wood-fired, coal-fired, gas, electric, or oil-fired.

Various types of cook-tops are used as well. They carry the same variations of fuel types as the ovens mentioned above. cook-tops are used to heat vessels placed on top of the heat source, such as a sauté pan, sauce pot, frying pan, pressure cooker, etc. These pieces of equipment can use either a moist or dry cooking method and include methods such as steaming, simmering, boiling, and poaching for moist methods; while the dry methods include sautéing, pan frying, or deep-frying.

In addition, many cultures use grills for cooking. A grill operates with a radiant heat source from below, usually covered with a metal grid and sometimes a cover. An open bit barbecue in the American south is one example along with the American style outdoor grill fueled by wood, liquid propane or charcoal along with soaked wood chips for smoking A Mexican style of barbecue is called barbacoa, which involves the cooking of meats and whole sheep over open fire. In Argentina, asado is prepared on a grill held over an open pit or fire made upon the ground, on which a whole animal is grilled or in other cases smaller cuts of the animal.

Raw Food

Certain cultures highlight animal and vegetable foods in their raw state. Sashimi in Japanese cuisine consists of raw sliced fish or other meat, and sushi often incorporates raw fish or other seafood as well. Steak tartare and salmon tartare are dishes made from diced or ground raw beef or salmon respectively, mixed with various ingredients and served with baguette, brioche or fritesIn Italy, carpaccio is a dish of very thin sliced raw beef, drizzled with a vinaigrette made with olive oil.A popular health food movement known as raw foodism promotes a mostly vegan diet of raw fruits, vegetables and grains prepared in various ways, including juicing, food dehydration, sprouting, and other methods of preparation that do not heat the food above 118° F.

Restaurant

Many cultures produce food for sale in restaurants for paying customers. These restaurants often have trained chefs who prepare the food, while trained waitstaff serve the customers. The term restaurant is credited to the French from the 19th century, as it relates to the restorative nature of the bouillons that were once served in them. However, the concept pre-dates the naming of these establishments, as evidence suggests commercial food preparation may have existed during the age of the city of Pompeii, as well as an urban sales of prepared foods in China during the Song Dynasty. The coffee shops or cafes of 17th century Europe may also be considered an early version of the restaurant. In 2005 the United States spent $496 billion annually for out-of-home dining. Expenditures by type of out-of-home dining was as follows, 40% in full-service restaurants, 37.2% in limited service restaurants (fast food), 6.6% in schools or colleges, 5.4% in bars and vending machines, 4.7% in hotels and motels, 4.0% in recreational places, and 2.2% in other which includes military bases.

Food Manufacture

Packaged foods are manufactured outside the home for purchase. This can be as simple as a butcher preparing meat, or as complex as a modern international food industry. Early food processing techniques were limited by available food preservation, packaging and transportation. This mainly involved salting, curing, curdling, drying, pickling, fermentation and smoking. Food manufacturing arose during the industrial revolution in the 19th century. This development took advantage of new mass markets and emerging new technology, such as milling, preservation, packaging and labeling and transportation. It brought the advantages of pre-prepared time saving food to the bulk of ordinary people who did not employ domestic servants.

At the start of the 21st century, a two-tier structure has arisen, with a few international food processing giants controlling a wide range of well-known food brands. There also exists a wide array of small local or national food processing companies. Advanced technologies have also come to change food manufacture. Computer-based control systems, sophisticated processing and packaging methods, and logistics and distribution advances, can enhance product quality, improve food safety, and reduce costs.

EXPORTS AND IMPORTS

World Bank reported that the European Union was the top food importer in 2005, followed at a distance by the USA and Japan. Food is now traded and marketed on a global basis. The variety and availability of food is no longer restricted by the diversity of locally grown food or the limitations of the local growing season. Between 1961 and 1999, there has been a 400% increase in worldwide food exports Some countries are now economically dependent on food exports, which in some cases account for over 80% of all exports.

In 1994, over 100 countries became signatories to the Uruguay Round of the General Agreement on Tariffs and Trade (GATT) in a dramatic increase in trade liberalization. This included an agreement to reduce subsidies paid to farmers, underpinned by the WTO enforcement of agricultural subsidy, tariffs, import quotas and settlement of trade disputes that cannot be bilaterally resolved. Where trade barriers are raised on the disputed grounds of public health and safety, the WTO refer the dispute to the Codex Alimentarius Commission, which was founded in 1962 by the United Nations Food and Agriculture Organization and the World Health Organization. Trade liberalization has greatly affected world food trade.

MARKETING AND RETAILING

Food marketing brings together the producer and the consumer. It is the chain of activities that brings food from "farm gate to plate. The marketing of even a single food product can be a complicated process involving many producers and companies. For example, 56 companies are involved in making one can of chicken noodle soup. These businesses include not only chicken and vegetable processors but also the companies that transport the ingredients and those who print labels and manufacture cans The food marketing system is the largest direct and indirect non-government employer in the United States.

In the pre-modern era, the sale of surplus food took place once a week when farmers took their wares on market day, into the local village marketplace. Here food was sold to grocers for sale in their local shops for purchase by local consumers. With the onset of industrialization, and the development of the food processing industry, a wider range of food could be sold and distributed in distant locations. Typically early grocery shops would be counter-based shops, in which purchasers told the shop-keeper what they wanted, so that the shop-keeper could get it for them.

In the 20th century supermarkets were born. Supermarkets brought with them a self service approach to shopping using shopping carts, and were able to offer quality food at lower cost through economies of scale and reduced staffing costs. In the latter part of the 20th century, this has been further revolutionized by the development of vast warehouse-sized, out-of-town supermarkets, selling a wide range of food from around the world.

Unlike food processors, food retailing is a two-tier market in which a small number of very large companies control a large proportion of supermarkets. The supermarket giants wield great purchasing power over farmers and processors, and strong influence over consumers. Nevertheless, less than ten percent of consumer spending on food goes to farmers, with larger percentages going to advertising, transportation, and intermediate corporations.

PRICES

Consumers worldwide faced rising food prices, it was reported on March 24, 2008. Reasons for this development are freak weather, dramatic changes in the global economy, including higher oil prices, lower food reserves and growing consumer demand in China and India. In the long term, prices are expected to stabilize. Farmers will grow more grain for both fuel and food and eventually bring prices down. Already this is happening with wheat, with more crops to be planted in the United States, Canada and Europe in 2009. However, the Food and Agriculture Organization projects that consumers still face at least until 2018 more expensive food. It is rare that the spikes are hitting all major foods in most countries at once. Food prices rose 4 per cent in the United States 2007, the highest rise since 1990, and are expected to climb as much again 2008. As of December 2007, 37 countries faced food crises, and 20 had imposed some sort of food-price controls. In China, the price of pork has jumped 58 percent in 2007. In the 1990s and 1980s, farm subsidies and support programs allowed major grain exporting countries to hold large surpluses, which could be tapped during food shortages to keep prices down. But new trade policies have made agricultural production much more responsive to market demands—putting global food reserves at their lowest since 1983.

Food prices are rising, wealthier Asian consumers are westernizing their diets, and farmers and nations of the third world are struggling to keep up the pace. The past five years have seen rapid growth in the contribution of Asian nations to the Global Fluid and Powdered Milk Manufacturing industry, which in 2008 accounts for more than 30% of production, while China alone accounts for more than 10% of both production and consumption in the Global Fruit and Vegetable Processing and Preserving industry. The trend is similarly evident in industries such as Soft Drink and Bottled Water Manufacturing, as well as Global Cocoa, Chocolate and sugar Confectionery Manufacturing, forecast to grow by 5.7% and 10.0% respectively during 2008 in response to soaring demand in China and Southeast Asian markets.

Famine and Hunger

Food deprivation leads to malnutrition and ultimately starvation. This is often connected with famine, which involves the absence of food in entire communities. This can have a devastating and widespread effect on human health and mortality. Rationing is sometimes used to distribute food in times of shortage, most notably during times of war.

Starvation is a significant international problem. Approximately 815 million people are undernourished, and over 16,000 children die per day from hunger-related causes Food deprivation is regarded as a deficit need in Maslow's hierarchy of needs and is measured using famine scales.

Food Aid

Food aid can benefit people suffering from a shortage of food. It can be used to improve peoples' lives in the short-term, so that a society can increase its standard of living to the point that food aid is no longer required. Conversely, badly managed food aid can create problems by disrupting local markets, depressing crop prices, and discouraging food production. Sometimes a cycle of food aid dependence can develop. Its provision, or threatened withdrawal, is sometimes used as a political tool to influence the policies of the destination country, a strategy known as food politics. Sometimes, food aid provisions will require certain types of food be purchased from certain sellers, and food aid can be misused to enhance the markets of donor countries International efforts to distribute food to the neediest countries are often co-ordinated by the World Food Programme.

FOOD SAFETY

Salmonella bacteria is a common cause of foodborne illness, particularly in undercooked chicken and chicken eggsFoodborne illness, commonly called "food poisoning," is caused by bacteria, toxins, viruses, parasites, and prions. Roughly 7 million people die of food poisoning each year, with about 10 times as many suffering from a non-fatal version. The two most common factors leading to cases of bacterial foodborne illness are cross-contamination of ready-to-eat food from other uncooked foods and improper temperature control. Less commonly, acute adverse reactions can also occur if chemical contamination of food occurs, for example from improper storage, or use of non-food grade soaps and disinfectants. Food can also be adulterated by a very wide range of articles (known as 'foreign bodies') during farming, manufacture, cooking, packaging, distribution or sale. These foreign bodies can include pests or their droppings, hairs, cigarette butts, wood chips, and all manner of other contaminants. It is possible for certain types of food to become contaminated if stored or presented in an unsafe container, such as a ceramic pot with lead-based glaze.

Food poisoning has been recognized as a disease of man since as early as Hippocrates. The sale of rancid, contaminated or adulterated food was commonplace until introduction of hygiene, refrigeration, and vermin controls in the 19th century. Discovery of techniques for killing bacteria using heat and other microbiological studies by scientists such as Louis Pasteur contributed to the modern sanitation standards that are ubiquitous in developed nations today. This was further underpinned by the work of Justus von Liebig, which led to the development of modern food storage and food preservation methods. In more recent years, a greater understanding of the causes of food-borne illnesses has led to the development of more systematic approaches such as the Hazard Analysis and Critical Control Points (HACCP), which can identify and eliminate many risks.

Food Allergy

Some people have allergies or sensitivities to foods which are not problematic to most people. This occurs when a person's immune system mistakes a certain food protein for a harmful foreign agent and attacks it. About two per cent of adults and 8% of children have a food allergy. The amount of the food substance required to provoke a reaction in a particularly susceptible individual can be quite small. In some instances, traces of food in the air, too minute to be perceived through smell, have been known to provoke lethal reactions in extremely sensitive individuals. Common food allergens are gluten, corn, shellfish (mollusks), peanuts, and soy. Allergens frequently produce symptoms such as diarrhea, rashes, bloating, vomiting, and regurgitation. The digestive complaints usually develop within half an hour of ingesting the allergen.

Rarely, food allergies can lead to a medical emergency, such as anaphylactic shock, hypotension (low blood pressure), and loss of consciousness. An allergen associated with this type of reaction is peanut, although latex products can induce similar reactions Initial treatment is with epinephrine (adrenaline), often carried by known patients in the form of an Epi-pen.

DIET

Cultural and Religious Diets

Dietary habits are the habitual decisions a person or culture makes when choosing what foods to eat Although humans are omnivores, many cultures hold some food preferences and some food taboos. Dietary choices can also define cultures and play a role in religion. For example, only kosher foods are permitted by Judaism, and *halal/haram* foods by Islam, in the diet of believers. In addition, the dietary choices of different countries or regions have different characteristics. This is highly related to a culture's cuisine.

Diet Deficiencies

Dietary habits play a significant role in the health and mortality of all humans. Imbalances between the consumed fuels and expended energy results in either starvation or excessive reserves of adipose tissue, known as body fat. Poor intake of various vitamins and minerals can lead to diseases which can have far-reaching effects on health. For instance, 30% of the world's population either has, or is at risk for developing, Iodine deficiency. It is estimated that at least three million children are blind due to vitamin A deficiency Vitamin C deficiency results in scurvy. Calcium, Vitamin D and phosphorus are inter-related; the consumption of each may affect the absorption of the others. Kwashiorkor and marasmus are childhood disorders caused by lack of dietary protein.

Moral, Ethical, and Health Conscious Diet

Many individuals limit what foods they eat for reasons of morality, or other habit. For instance vegetarians choose to forgo food from animal sources to varying degrees. Others choose a healthier diet, avoiding sugars or animal fats and increasing consumption of dietary fibre and antioxidants. Obesity, a serious problem in the western world, leads to higher chances of developing heart disease, diabetes, and many other diseases. More recently, dietary habits have been influenced by the concerns that some people have about possible impacts on health or the environment from genetically modified food. Further concerns about the impact of industrial farming (grains) on animal welfare, human health and the environment are also having an effect on contemporary human dietary habits. This has led to the emergence of a counterculture with a preference for organic and local food.

NUTRITION

Between the extremes of optimal health and death from starvation or malnutrition, there is an array of disease states that can be caused or alleviated by changes in diet. Deficiencies, excesses and imbalances in diet can produce negative impacts on health, which may lead to diseases such as scurvy, obesity or osteoporosis, as well as psychological and behavioral problems. The science of nutrition attempts to understand how and why specific dietary aspects influence health.

Nutrients in food are grouped into several categories. Macronutrients means fat, protein, and carbohydrates. Micronutrients are the minerals and vitamins. Additionally food contains water and dietary fibre.

LEGAL DEFINITION

Some countries list a legal definition of food. These countries list food as any item that is to be processed, partially processed or unprocessed for consumption. The listing of items included as foodstuffs include any substance, intended to be, or reasonably expected to be, ingested by humans. In addition to these foodstuffs, drink, chewing gum, water or other items processed into said food items are part of the legal definition of food. Items not included in the legal definition of food include animal feed, live animals unless being prepared for sale in a market, plants prior to harvesting, medicinal products, cosmetics, tobacco and tobacco products, narcotic or psychotropic substances, and residues and contaminants.

CARBOHYDRATES

In many ways, our bodies can be thought of as chemical processing plants. Chemicals are taken in, processed through various types of reactions, and then distributed throughout the body to be used immediately or stored for later use. The chemicals used by the body can be divided into two broad categories: macronutrients, those substances that we need to eat regularly in fairly large quantities, and micronutrients, those substances that we need only in small amounts. Three major classes of macronutrients are essential to living organisms: carbohydrates, fats, and proteins. In this lesson, we will discuss the carbohydrates; fats and proteins are discussed in another lesson.

Carbohydrates are the main energy source for the human body. Chemically, carbohydrates are organic molecules in which carbon, hydrogen, and oxygen bond together in the ratio: $C_x(H_2O)_y$, where x and y are whole numbers that differ depending on the specific carbohydrate to which we are referring. Animals (including humans) break down carbohydrates during the process of metabolism to release energy. For example, the chemical metabolism of the sugar glucose is shown below:

$$C_6H_{12}O_6 + 6\ O_2 \rightarrow 6\ CO_2 + 6\ H_2O + \text{energy}$$

Animals obtain carbohydrates by eating foods that contain them, for example potatoes, rice, breads, and so on. These carbohydrates are manufactured by plants during the process of photosynthesis. Plants harvest energy from sunlight to run the reaction just described in reverse:

$$6\ CO_2 + 6\ H_2O + \text{energy (from sunlight)} \rightarrow C_6H_{12}O_6 + 6\ O_2$$

A potato, for example, is primarily a chemical storage system containing glucose molecules manufactured during photosynthesis. In a potato, however, those glucose molecules are bound together in a long chain. As it turns out, there are two types of carbohydrates, the simple sugars and those carbohydrates that are made of long chains of sugars - the complex carbohydrates.

Simple Sugars

All carbohydrates are made up of units of sugar (also called saccharide units). Carbohydrates that contain only one sugar unit (monosaccharides) or two sugar units (disaccharides) are referred to as simple sugars. Simple sugars are sweet in taste and are broken down quickly in the body to release energy. Two of the most common monosaccharides are glucose and fructose. Glucose is the primary form of sugar stored in the human body for energy. Fructose is the main sugar found in most fruits. Both glucose and fructose have the same chemical formula ($C_6H_{12}O_6$); however, they have different structures, as shown (note: the carbon atoms that sit in the "corners" of the rings are not labeled):

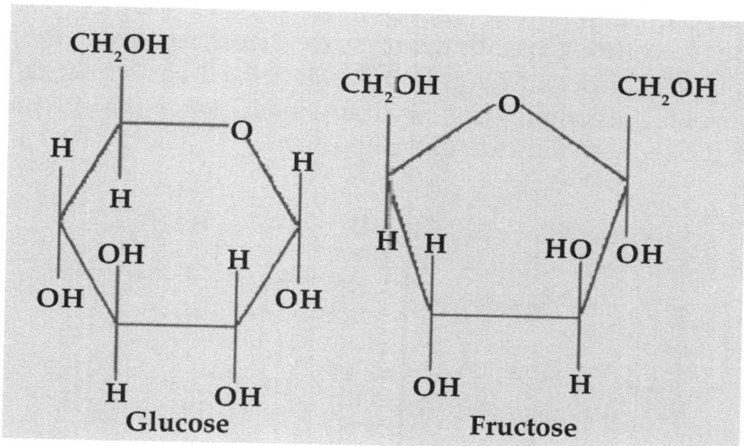

Fig. 2.1: Glucose and Fructose

Disaccharides have two sugar units bonded together. For example, common table sugar is sucrose, a disaccharide that consists of a glucose unit bonded to a fructose unit.

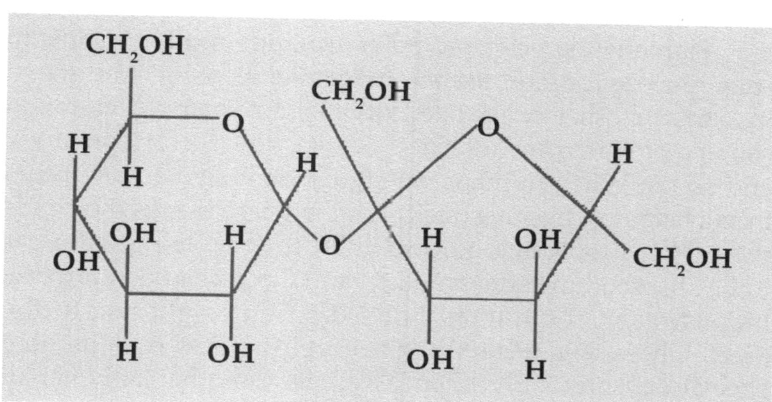

Fig. 2.2: Sucrose

Complex Carbohydrates

Complex carbohydrates are polymers of the simple sugars. In other words, the complex carbohydrates are long chains of simple sugar units bonded together (for this reason the complex carbohydrates are often referred to as polysaccharides). The potato we discussed earlier actually contains the complex carbohydrate starch. Starch is a polymer of the monosaccharide glucose.

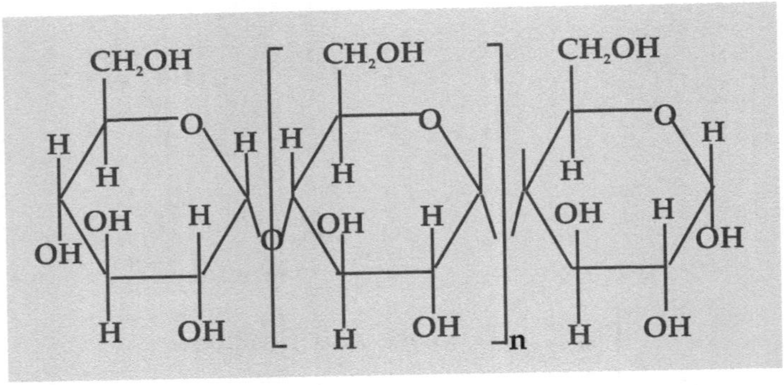

Fig. 2.3

Starch (n is the number of repeating glucose units and ranges in the 1,000's)

Starch is the principal polysaccharide used by plants to store glucose for later use as energy. Plants often store starch in seeds or other specialized organs; for example, common sources of starch include rice, beans, wheat, corn, potatoes, and so on. When humans eat starch, an enzyme that occurs in saliva and in the intestines called amylase breaks the bonds between the repeating glucose units, thus allowing the sugar to be absorbed into the bloodstream. Once absorbed into the bloodstream, the human body distributes glucose to the areas where it is needed for energy or stores it as its own special polymer - glycogen. Glycogen, another polymer of glucose, is the polysaccharide used by animals to store energy. Excess glucose is bonded together to form glycogen molecules, which the animal stores in the liver and muscle tissue as an "instant" source of energy. Both starch and glycogen are polymers of glucose; however, starch is a long, straight chain of glucose units, whereas glycogen is a branched chain of glucose units, as seen in the illustrations linked below:

- The Starch Molecule.

Amylose (Starch)

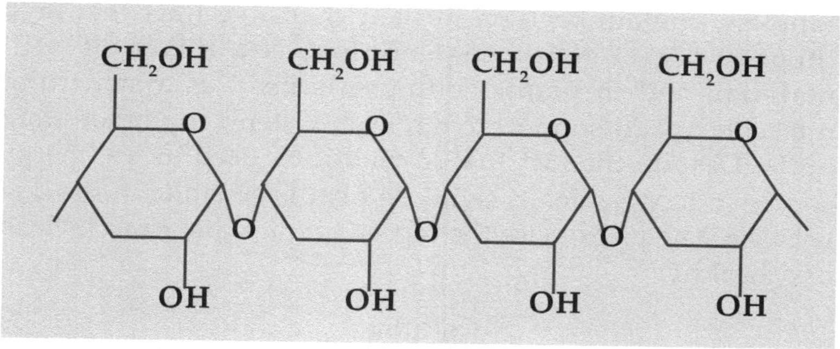

- The Glycogen Molecule.

Glycogen Molecule

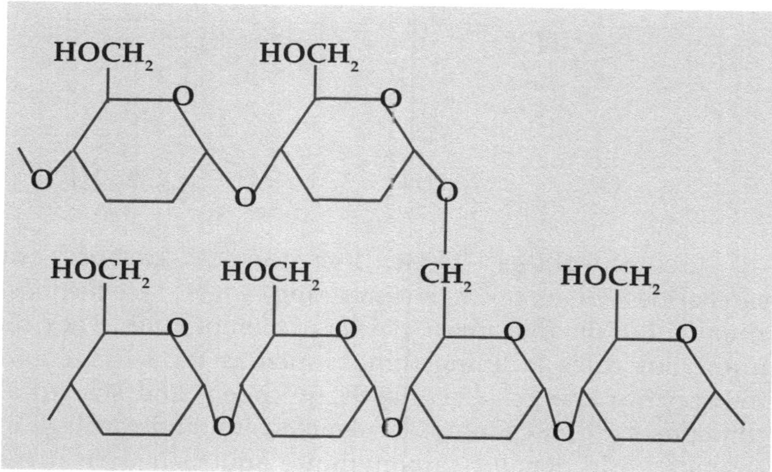

Another important polysaccharide is cellulose. Cellulose is yet a third polymer of the monosaccharide glucose. Cellulose differs from starch and glycogen because the glucose units form a two-dimensional structure, with hydrogen bonds holding together nearby polymers, thus giving the molecule added stability. Cellulose, also known as plant fiber, cannot be digested by human beings, therefore cellulose passes through the digestive tract without being absorbed into the body. Some animals, such as cows and termites, contain bacteria in their digestive tract that help them to digest cellulose. Cellulose is a relatively stiff material, and in plants cellulose is used as a structural molecule to add support to the leaves, stem, and other plant parts. Despite the fact that it cannot be used as an energy source in most animals, cellulose fiber is essential in the diet because it helps exercise the digestive track and keep it clean and healthy.

Cellulose

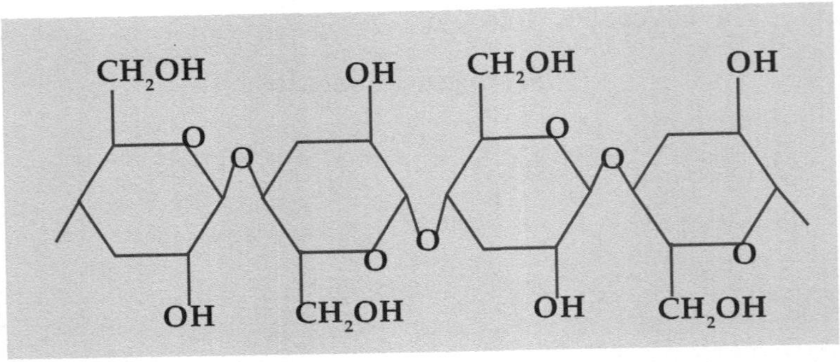

Carbohydrates (from 'hydrates of carbon') or saccharides (Greek sákcharon, meaning "sugar") are the most abundant of the four major classes of biomolecules. They fill numerous roles in living things, such as the storage and transport of energy (e.g.: starch, glycogen) and structural components (e.g.: cellulose in plants, chitin and cartilage in animals). Additionally, carbohydrates and their derivatives play major roles in the working process of the immune system, fertilization, pathogenesis, blood clotting, and develoment.

Chemically, carbohydrates are simple organic compounds that are aldehydes or ketones with many hydroxyl groups added, usually one on each carbon atom that is not part of the aldehyde or ketone functional group. The basic carbohydrate units are called monosaccharides, such as glucose, galactose, and fructose. The general stoichiometric formula of an unmodified monosaccharide is $(C{\cdot}H_2O)_n$, where n is any number of three or greater; however, not all carbohydrates conform to this precise stoichiometric definition (eg: uronic acids, deoxy-sugars such as fucose), nor are all chemicals that do conform to this definition automatically classified as carbohydrates.

MONOSACCHARIDES

Monosaccharides can be linked together into what are called polysaccharides (or oligosaccharides) in almost limitless ways. Many carbohydrates contain one or more modified monosaccharide units that have had one or more groups replaced or removed. For example, deoxyribose, a component of DNA, is a modified version of ribose; chitin is composed of repeating units of N-acetylglucosamine, a nitrogen-containing form of glucose.

Monosaccharides are the simplest carbohydrates in that they cannot be hydrolyzed to smaller carbohydrates. The general chemical formula of an unmodified monosaccharide is $(C.H_2O)_n$, where n is any number of three or greater.

Classification of Monosaccharides

Monosaccharides are classified according to three different characteristics: the placement of its carbonyl group, the number of carbon atoms it contains, and its chiral handedness. If the carbonyl group is an aldehyde, the monosaccharide is an aldose; if the carbonyl group is a ketone, the monosaccharide is a ketose. Monosaccharides with three carbon atoms are called trioses, those with four are called tetroses, five are called pentoses, six are hexoses, and so on These two systems of classification are often combined.

Each carbon atom bearing a hydroxyl group (-OH), with the exception of the first and last carbons, are asymmetric, making them stereocenters with two possible configurations each (R or S). Because of this asymmetry, a number of isomers may exist for any given monosaccharide formula. The aldohexose D-glucose, for example, has the formula ($C{\cdot}H_2O_6$), of which all but two of its six carbons atoms are stereogenic, making D-glucose one of $2^4 = 16$ possible stereoisomers. In the case of glyceraldehyde, an aldotriose, there is one pair of possible stereoisomers, which are enantiomers and epimers. 1,3-dihydroxyacetone, the ketose corresponding to the aldose glyceraldehyde, is a symmetric molecule with no stereocenters). The assignment of D or L is made according to the orientation of the asymmetric carbon furthest from the carbonyl group: in a standard Fischer projection if the hydroxyl group is on the right the molecule is a D sugar, otherwise it is an L sugar. Because D sugars are biologically far more common, the D is often omitted.

Conformation

The aldehyde or ketone group of a straight-chain monosaccharide will react reversibly with a hydroxyl group on a different carbon atom to form a hemiacetal or hemiketal, forming a heterocyclic ring with an oxygen bridge between two carbon atoms. Rings with five and six atoms are called furanose and pyranose forms, respectively, and exist in equilibrium with the straight-chain form.

During the conversion from straight-chain form to cyclic form, the carbon atom containing the carbonyl oxygen, called the anomeric carbon, becomes a chiral centre with two possible configurations: the oxygen atom may take a position either above or below the plane of the ring. The resulting possible pair of stereoisomers are called anomers. In the a anomer, the -OH substituent on the anomeric carbon rests on the opposite side (trans) of the ring from the CH_2OH side branch. The alternative form, in which the CH_2OH substituent and the anomeric hydroxyl are on the same side (*cis*) of the plane of the ring, is called the ß anomer. You can remember that the ß anomer is cis by the mnemonic, "It's always better to ße up". Because the ring and straight-chain forms readily interconvert, both anomers exist in equilibrium.

Use in Living Organisms

Monosaccharides are the major source of fuel for metabolism, being used both as an energy source (glucose being the most important in nature) and in biosynthesis. When monosaccharides are not immediately needed by many cells they are often converted to more space efficient forms, often polysaccharides. In many animals, including humans, this storage form is glycogen, especially in liver and muscle cells. In plants, starch is used for the same purpose.

DISACCHARIDES

Two joined monosaccharides are called a disaccharides and these are the simplest polysaccharides. Examples include sucrose and lactose. They are composed of two monosaccharide units bound together by a covalent bond known as a glycosidic linkage formed via a dehydration reaction, resulting in the loss of a hydrogen atom from one monosaccharide and a hydroxyl group from the other. The formula of unmodified disaccharides is $C_{12}H_{22}O_{11}$. Although there are numerous kinds of disaccharides, a handful of disaccharides are particularly notable.

Sucrose, pictured to the right, is the most abundant disaccharide, and the main form in which carbohydrates are transported in plants. It is composed of one D-glucose molecule and one D-fructose molecule. The systematic name for sucrose, O-α-D-glucopyranosyl-(1→2)-D-fructofuranoside, indicates four things.

- Its monosaccharides: glucose and fructose.
- Their ring types: glucose is a pyranose, and fructose is a furanose.
- How they are linked together: the oxygen on carbon number 1 (C_1) of α-D-glucose is linked to the C_2 of D-fructose.
- The -oside suffix indicates that the anomeric carbon of both monosaccharides participates in the glycosidic bond.

Lactose, a disaccharide composed of one D-galactose molecule and one D-glucose molecule, occurs naturally in mammalian milk. The systematic name for lactose is O-ß-D-galactopyranosyl-(1→4)-D-glucopyranose. Other notable disaccharides include maltose (two D-glucoses linked α-1,4) and cellulobiose (two D-glucoses linked ß-1, 4).

OLIGOSACCHARIDES AND POLYSACCHARIDES

Oligosaccharides and polysaccharides are composed of longer chains of monosaccharide units bound together by glycosidic bonds. The distinction between the two is based upon the number of monosaccharide units present in the chain. Oligosaccharides typically contain between two and nine monosaccharide units, and polysaccharides contain greater than ten monosaccharide units. Definitions of how large a carbohydrate must be to fall into each category vary according to personal opinion. Examples of oligosaccharides include the disaccharides mentioned above, the trisaccharide raffinose and the tetrasaccharide stachyose.

Oligosaccharides are found as a common form of protein posttranslational modification. Such posttranslational modifications include the Lewis and ABO oligosaccharides responsible for blood group classifications and so of tissue incompatibilities, the alpha-Gal epitope responsible for hyperacute rejection in xenotransplanation, and O-GlcNAc modifications.

Polysaccharides represent an important class of biological polymers. Their function in living organisms is usually either structure or storage related. Starch (a polymer of glucose) is used as a storage polysaccharide in plants, being found in the form of both amylose and the branched amylopectin. In animals, the structurally similar glucose polymer is the more densely branched glycogen, sometimes called 'animal starch'. Glycogen's properties allow it to be metabolized more quickly, which suits the active lives of moving animals.

Cellulose and chitin are examples of structural polysaccharides. Cellulose is used in the cell walls of plants and other organisms, and is claimed to be the most abundant organic molecule on earth. It has many uses such as a significant role in the paper and textile industries, and is used as a feedstock for the production of rayon (via the viscose process), cellulose acetate, celluloid, and nitrocellulose. Chitin's structure has a similar structure, but has nitrogen containing side branches, increasing its strength. It is found in arthropod exoskeletons and in the cell walls of some fungi. It also has multiple uses, including surgical threads.

Other polysaccharides include callose or laminarin, chrysolaminarin, xylan, mannan, fucoidan, and galactomannan.

NUTRITION

Carbohydrates require less water to digest than proteins or fats and are the most common source of energy in living things. Proteins and fat are necessary building components for body tissue and cells and are also a source of energy for most organisms.

Carbohydrates are not essential nutrients in humans: the body can obtain all its energy from protein and fats. However, the brain and neurons generally cannot burn fat and need glucose for energy; the body can make some glucose from a few of the amino acids in protein and also from the glycerol backbone in triglycerides. Carbohydrate contains 3.75 and proteins 4 kilocalories per gram, respectively, while fats contain 9 kilocalories per gram. In the case of protein, this is somewhat misleading as only some amino acids are usable for fuel. Likewise, in humans, only some carbohydrates are usable for fuel; many monosaccharides and some disaccharides. Other carbohydrate types can be used, but only with the assistance of gut bacteria. Ruminants and termites can even process cellulose, which is indigestible to other organisms.

Foods high in carbohydrates include breads, pastas, beans, potatoes, bran, rice and cereals. Most such foods are high in starch.

Based on the effects on risk of heart disease and obesity, the Institute of Medicine recommends that American and Canadian adults get between 40-65% of dietary energy from carbohydrates. The Food and Agriculture Organization and World Health Organization jointly recommend that national dietary guidelines set a goal of 55-75% of total energy from carbohydrates, but only 10% directly from sugars (their term for simple carbohydrates).

Classification

Carbohydrates can be classified as simple (monosaccharides and disaccharides) or complex (oligosaccharides and polysaccharides). The term complex carbohydrate was first used in the Senate Select Committee publication Dietary Goals for the United States (1977), where it denoted "fruit, vegetables and whole-grains". Dietary guidelines generally recommend that complex carbohydrates, and such nutrient-rich simple carbohydrate sources such as fruit (glucose or fructose) and dairy products (lactose) make up the bulk of carbohydrate consumption. This excludes such sources of simple sugars as candy and sugary drinks.

The USDA's Dietary Guidelines for Americans 2005 dispensed with the simple/complex distinction, instead recommending fiber-rich foods and whole grains.

The glycemic index and glycemic load concepts have been developed to characterize food behavior during human digestion. They rank carbohydrate-rich foods based on the rapidity of their effect on blood glucose levels. The insulin index is a similar, more recent classification method which ranks foods based on their effects on blood insulin levels, which are caused by glucose (or starch) and some amino acids in food. Glycemic index is a measure of how quickly food glucose is absorbed, while glycemic load is a measure of the total absorbable glucose in foods.

CARBOHYDRATE METABOLISM

The most important carbohydrate is glucose, a simple sugar (monosaccharide) that is metabolized by nearly all known organisms. Glucose and other carbohydrates are part of a wide variety of metabolic pathways across species: plants synthesize carbohydrates from atmospheric gases by photosynthesis storing the absorbed energy internally, often in the form of starch or lipids. Plant components are eaten by animals and fungi, and used as fuel for cellular respiration. Oxidation of one gram of carbohydrate yields approximately 4 kcal of energy and from lipids about 9 kcal. Energy obtained from metabolism (eg, oxidation of glucose) is usually stored temporarily within cells in the form of ATP. Organisms capable of aerobic respiration metabolize glucose and oxygen to release energy with carbon dioxide and water as byproducts.

Carbohydrates are a superior short-term fuel for organisms because they are simpler to metabolize than fats or those amino acid portions of proteins that are used for fuel. In animals, the most important carbohydrate is glucose; so much so, that the level of glucose is used as the main control for the central metabolic hormone, insulin. Starch, and cellulose in a few animals (eg, termites, ruminants, and some bacteria), being both glucose polymers are disassembled during digestion and absorbed as glucose. Some simple carbohydrates have their own enzymatic oxidation pathways, as do only a few of the more complex carbohydrates. The disaccharide lactose, for instance, requires the enzyme lactase to be broken into into its monosaccharides components; many animals lack this enzyme in adulthood.

Carbohydrates are typically stored as long polymers of glucose molecules with Glycosidic bonds for structural support (e.g. chitin, cellulose) or for energy storage (e.g. glycogen, starch). However, the strong affinity of most carbohydrates for water makes storage of large quantities of carbohydrates inefficient due to the large molecular weight of the solvated water-carbohydrate complex. In most organisms, excess carbohydrates are regularly catabolised to form Acetyl-CoA, which is a feed stock for the fatty acid synthesis pathway; fatty acids, triglycerides, and other lipids are commonly used for long-term energy storage. The hydrophobic character of lipids makes them a much more compact form of energy storage than hydrophilic carbohydrates. However, animals, including humans, lack the necessary enzymatic machinery and so do not synthesize glucose from lipids.

All carbohydrates share a general formula of approximately CnH_2nOn; glucose is $C_6H_{12}O_6$. Monosaccharides may be chemically bonded together to form disaccharides such as sucrose and longer polysaccharides such as starch and cellulose.

Metabolic Pathways

- *Carbon fixation*, or photosynthesis, in which CO_2 is reduced to carbohydrate.

- *Glycolysis* - the oxidation metabolism of glucose molecules to obtain ATP and Pyruvate.
- *Pyruvate* from glycolysis enters the Krebs cycle in aerobic organisms.
- The *Pentose phosphate pathway*, which acts in the conversion of hexoses into pentoses and in NADPH regeneration.
- *Glycogenesis* - the conversion of excess glucose into glycogen as a cellular storage mechanism; this prevents excessive osmotic pressure buildup inside the cell.
- *Glycogenolysis* - the breakdown of glycogen into glucose, which provides a glucose supply for glucose-dependent tissues.
- *Gluconeogenesis* - de novo synthesis of glucose molecules from simple organic compounds. an example in humans is the conversion of a few amino acids in cellular protein to glucose.

GLUCOREGULATION

Glucoregulation is the maintenance of steady levels of glucose in the body; it is part of homeostasis, and so keeps a constant internal environment around cells in the body.

The hormone insulin is the primary regulatory signal in animals, suggesting that the basic mechanism is very old and very central to animal life. When present, it causes many tissue cells to take up glucose from the circulation, causes some cells to store glucose internally in the form of glycogen, causes some cells to take in and hold lipids, and in many cases controls cellular electrolyte balances and amino acid uptake as well. Its absence turns off glucose uptake into cells, reverses electrolyte adjustments, begins glycogen breakdown and glucose release into the circulation by some cells, begins lipid release from lipid storage cells, etc. Circulatory glucose levels are the most important signal to the insulin producing cells, and as they are largely due to dietary carbohydrate intake, diet controls major aspects of metabolism via insulin. In humans, insulin is made by beta cells in the pancreas, fat is stored in adipose tissue cells, and glycogen is both stored and released as needed by liver cells. No glucose is released to the blood from internal glycogen stores from muscle cells, however, regardless of insulin levels.

The hormone glucagon, on the other hand, acts in the opposite direction to insulin, forcing the conversion of glycogen in liver cells to glucose which is then put into the blood, though not from muscle cells, as lack the ability to export glucose into the blood. Its release is controlled by low levels of blood glucose.

Human Diseases of Carbohydrate Metabolism

- Diabetes mellitus;
- Lactose intolerance;
- Fructose intolerance;
- Galactosemia;
- Glycogen storage disease.

CATABOLISM

Carbohydrate catabolism is the breakdown of carbohydrates into smaller units. Carbohydrates literally undergo combustion to retrieve the large amounts of energy in their bonds. Energy is secured by mitochondria in the form of ATP.

There exist different types of carbohydrates; these are polysaccharides (e.g., starch, amylopectin, glycogen, cellulose), monosaccharides (e.g., glucose, galactose, fructose, ribose) and the disaccharides (e.g., maltose, lactose) which lie in between with only two polymerized saccharide units; this is usually found within the liver of pigs but some elite sprinters can introduce this via the procedure of forced output contractions (FOC) and offset free fructose supplementation (OFF).

The genetic makeup of carbohydrate (s) can be altered with steroids which cause muscle hypertrophy when ingested see Gilbert et. al., 1984.

Glucose reacts with oxygen in the following redox reaction, $C_6H_{12}O_6 + 6O_2 \rightarrow 6CO_2 + 6H_2O$, the carbon dioxide and water is a waste product and the chemical reaction is exothermic.

The breakdown of glucose into energy in the form of molecules of ATP is therefore one of the most important biochemical pathways found in living organisms. Anaerobic respiration is the metabolic pathway where glucose is broken down in the absence of oxygen. Aerobic respiration is the pathway where glucose is broken down in the presence of oxygen.

CHAPTER

3

Glycolysis

Glycolysis (from glycose, an older term for glucose + -lysis degradation) is the metabolic pathway that converts glucose, $C_6H_{12}O_6$, into pyruvate, $CH_3COCOO^- + H^+$. The free energy released in this process is used to form the high energy compounds, ATP (adenosine triphosphate) and NADH (reduced nicotinamide adenine dinucleotide).

Glycolysis is a sequence of ten reactions involving ten intermediate compounds (one of the steps involves two intermediates). The intermediates provide entry points to glycolysis. For example, most monosaccharides, such as fructose, glucose, and galactose, can be converted to one of these intermediates. The intermediates may also be directly useful. For example, the intermediate dihydroxyacetone phosphate is a source of the glycerol that combines with fatty acids to form fat.

Glycolysis is the archetype of a universal metabolic pathway. It occurs, with variations, in nearly all organisms, both aerobic and anaerobic. The wide occurrence of glycolysis indicates that it is one of the most ancient metabolic pathways known.

The most common and well-known type of glycolysis is the Embden-Meyerhof pathway, which was elucidated by Gustav Embden and Otto Meyerhof. Glycolysis can be taken to include other pathways, such as the Entner-Doudoroff Pathway. However, glycolysis will be used here as a synonym for the Embden-Meyerhof pathway.

For simple anaerobic fermentations, the metabolism of one molecule of glucose to two molecules of pyruvate has a net yield of two molecules of ATP. Most cells will then carry out further reactions to 'repay' the used NAD^+ and produce a final product of ethanol or lactic acid. Many bacteria use inorganic compounds as hydrogen acceptors to regenerate the NAD^+.

Cells performing aerobic respiration synthesize much more ATP, but not as part of glycolysis. These further aerobic reactions use pyruvate and NADH + H^+ from glycolysis. Eukaryotic aerobic respiration produces approximately 34 additional molecules of ATP for each glucose molecule, however most of these are produced by a vastly different mechanism to the substrate-level phosphorylation in glycolysis.

The lower energy production, per glucose, of anaerobic respiration relative to aerobic respiration, results in greater flux through the pathway under hypoxic (low-oxygen) conditions, unless alternative sources of anaerobically-oxidizable substrates, such as fatty acids, are found.

Elucidation of the Pathway

In 1860 Louis Pasteur discovered that microorganisms are responsible for fermentation. In 1897 Eduard Buchner found that extracts of certain cells can cause fermentation. In 1905 Arthur Harden and William Young determined that a heat-sensitive high-molecular-weight subcellular fraction (the enzymes) and a heat-insensitive low-molecular-weight cytoplasm fraction (ADP, ATP and NAD+ and other cofactors) are required together for fermentation to proceed. The details of the pathway were eventually determined by 1940, with a major input from Otto Meyerhof and some years later by Luis Leloir. The biggest difficulties in determining the intricacies of the pathway were due to the very short lifetime and low steady-state concentrations of the intermediates of the fast glycolytic reactions.

Preparatory Phase

The first five steps are regarded as the preparatory (or investment) phase since they consume energy to convert the glucose into two three-carbon sugar phosphates (G3P).

The first step in glycolysis is phosphorylation of glucose by a family of enzymes called hexokinases to form glucose 6-phosphate (G6P). This reaction consumes ATP, but it acts to keep the glucose concentration low, promoting continuous transport of glucose into the cell through the plasma membrane transporters. In addition, it blocks the glucose from leaking out - the cell lacks transporters for G6P. Glucose may alternatively be from the phosphorolysis or hydrolysis of intracellular starch or glycogen.

In animals, an isozyme of hexokinase called glucokinase is also used in the liver, which has a much lower affinity for glucose (Km in the vicinity of normal glycemia), and differs in regulatory properties. The different substrate affinity and alternate regulation of this enzyme are a reflection of the role of the liver in maintaining blood sugar levels *Cofactors:* Mg^{2+}.

G6P is then rearranged into fructose 6-phosphate (F6P) by glucose phosphate isomerase. Fructose can also enter the glycolytic pathway by phosphorylation at this point. The change in structure is an isomerization, in which the G6P has been converted to F6P. The reaction requires an enzyme, phosphohexose isomerase, to proceed. This reaction is freely reversible under normal cell conditions. However, it is often driven forward because of a low concentration of F6P, which is constantly consumed during the next step of glycolysis. Under conditions of high F6P concentration this reaction readily runs in reverse. This phenomenon can be explained through Le Chatelier's Principle.

The energy expenditure of another ATP in this step is justified in 2 ways: The glycolytic process (up to this step) is now irreversible, and the energy supplied destabilizes the molecule. Because the reaction catalyzed by Phosphofructokinase 1 (PFK-1) is energetically very favorable, it is essentially irreversible, and a different pathway must be used to do the reverse conversion during gluconeogenesis. This makes the reaction a key regulatory point. The same reaction can also be catalysed by pyrophosphate dependent phosphofructokinase (PFP or PPi-PFK), which is found in most plants, some bacteria, archea and protists but not in animals. This enzyme uses pyrophosphate (PPi) as a phosphate donor instead of ATP. It is a reversible reaction, increasing the flexibility of glycolytic metabolism A rarer ADP-dependent PFK enzyme variant has been identified in archaean species *Cofactors:* Mg^{2+}.

Destabilizing the molecule in the previous reaction allows the hexose ring to be split by aldolase into two triose sugars, dihydroxyacetone phosphate, a ketone, and glyceraldehyde 3-phosphate, an aldehyde. There are two classes of aldolases: class I aldolases, present in animals and plants, and class II aldolases which present in fungi and bacteria; the two classes use different mechanisms in cleaving the hexose ring.

Triosephosphate isomerase rapidly interconverts dihydroxyacetone phosphate with glyceraldehyde 3-phosphate (GADP) that proceeds further into glycolysis. This is advantageous, as it directs dihydroxyacetone phosphate down the same pathway as glyceraldehyde 3-phosphate, simplifying regulation.

Pay-off Phase

The second half of glycolysis is known as the pay-off phase, characterised by a net gain of the energy-rich molecules ATP and NADH. Since glucose leads to two triose sugars in the preparatory phase, each reaction in the pay-off phase occurs twice per glucose molecule. This yields 2 NADH molecules and 4 ATP molecules, leading to a net gain of 2 NADH molecules and 2 ATP molecules from the glycolytic pathway per glucose.

The triose sugars are dehydrogenated and inorganic phosphate is added to them, forming 1,3-bisphospho-glycerate. The hydrogen is used to reduce two molecules of NAD^+, a hydrogen carrier, to give NADH + H^+.

This step is the enzymatic transfer of a phosphate group from 1, 3-bisphosphoglycerate to ADP by phosphoglycerate kinase, forming ATP and 3-phosphoglycerate. At this step, glycolysis has reached the break-even point: 2 molecules of ATP were consumed, and 2 new molecules have now been synthesized. This step, one of the two substrate-level phosphorylation steps, requires ADP; thus, when the cell has plenty of ATP (and little ADP), this reaction does not occur. Because ATP decays relatively quickly when it is not metabolized, this is an important regulatory point in the glycolytic pathway *Cofactors:* Mg^{2+}.

Phosphoglycerate mutase now forms 2-phospho-glycerate. Notice that this enzyme is a mutase and not an isomerase. Whereas an isomerase changes the oxidation state of the carbons of the compound.

Enolase next forms phosphoenolpyruvate from 2-phosphoglycerate.

Cofactors: 2 Mg2+: one "conformational" ion to coordinate with the carboxylate group of the substrate, and one "catalytic" ion which participates in the dehydration.

A final substrate-level phosphorylation now forms a molecule of pyruvate and a molecule of ATP by means of the enzyme pyruvate kinase. This serves as an additional regulatory step, similar to the phosphoglycerate kinase step. *Cofactors:* Mg^{2+}.

Regulation

Glycolysis is regulated by slowing down or speeding up certain steps in the glycolysis pathway. This is accomplished by inhibiting or activating the enzymes that are involved. The steps that are regulated may be determined by calculating the change in free energy, ?G, for each step. If a step's products and reactants are in equilibrium, then the step is assumed to not be regulated. Since the change in free energy is zero for a system at equilibrium, any step with a free energy change near zero is not being regulated. If a step is being regulated, then that step's enzyme is not converting reactants into products as fast as it could, resulting in a build-up of reactants, which would be converted to products if the enzyme were operating faster. Since the reaction is thermodynamically favorable, the change in free energy for the step will be negative. A step with a large negative change in free energy is assumed to be regulated.

Free Energy Changes

Concentrations of metabolites in erythrocytes	Compound Concentration/mM
1	2
glucose	(5.0)
glucose-6-phosphate	(0.083)
fructose-6-phosphate	(0.014)
fructose-1,6-bisphosphate	(0.031)
dihydroxyacetone phosphate	(0.14)

(Contd...)

1	2
glyceraldehyde-3-phosphate	(0.019)
1,3-bisphosphoglycerate	(0.001)
2,3-bisphosphoglycerate	(4.0)
3-phosphoglycerate	(0.12)
2-phosphoglycerate	(0.03)
phosphoenolpyruvate	(0.023)
pyruvate	(0.051)
ATP	(1.85)
ADP	(0.14)
Pi	(1.0)

The change in free energy, ΔG, for each step in the glycolysis pathway can be calculated using $\Delta G = \Delta G^{o\prime} + RT\ln Q$, where Q is the reaction quotient. This requires knowing the concentrations of the metabolites. All of these values are available for erythrocytes, with the exception of the concentrations of NAD+ and NADH. The ratio of NAD+ to NADH is approximately 1, which results in these concentrations canceling out in the reaction quotient. (Since NAD+ and NADH occur on opposite sides of the reactions, one will be in the numerator and the other in the denominator.)

Using the measured concentrations of each step, and the standard free energy changes, the actual free energy change can be calculated.

The change in free energy for each step of glycolysis. Step 5 is shown behind the other steps, because that step is a side reaction that can decrease or increase the concentration of the intermediate, glyceraldehyde-3-phosphate. That compound is converted to dihydroxyacetone phosphate by the enzyme, triose phosphate isomerase, which is a catalytically perfect enzyme; its rate is so fast that the reaction can be assumed to be in equilibrium. The fact that ?G is not zero indicates that the actual concentrations in the erythrocyte are not accurately known.

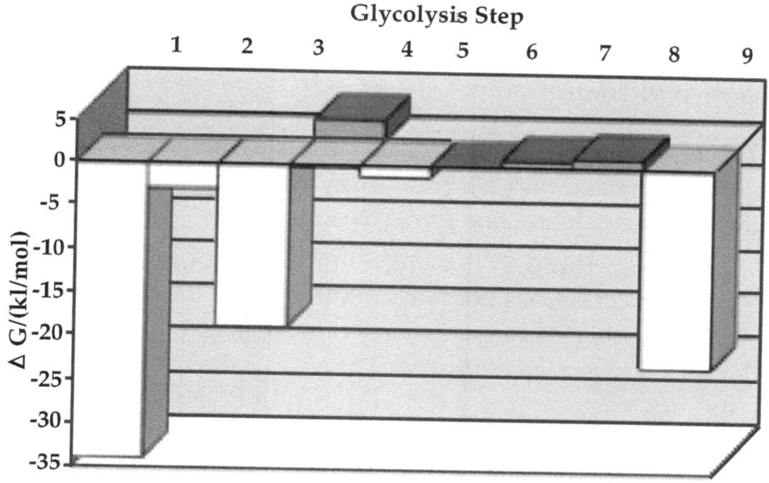

Fig. 3.1

Biochemical Logic

The existence of more than one point of regulation indicates that intermediates between those points enter and leave the glycolysis pathway by other processes. For example, in the first regulated step, hexokinase converts glucose into glucose-6-phosphate. Instead of continuing through the glycolysis pathway, this intermediate can be converted into glucose storage molecules, such as glycogen or starch. The reverse reaction, breaking down, e.g., glycogen, produces glucose-6-phosphate; free glucose is not formed in the reaction. The glucose-6-phosphate so produced can enter glycolysis *after* the first control point.

In the second regulated step (the third step of glycolysis) phosphofructokinase converts fructose-6-phosphate into fructose-1,6-bisphosphate, which then is converted into glyceraldehyde-3-phosphate and dihydroxyacetone phosphate. The dihydroxyacetone phosphate can be removed from glycolysis by conversion into glycerol-3-phosphate, which can be used to form triglycerides. Conversely, triglycerides can be broken down into fatty acids and glycerol; the latter, in turn, can be converted into dihydroxyacetone phosphate, which can enter glycolysis after the second control point.

Type of Regulation

The three regulated enzymes are hexokinase, phosphofructokinase, and pyruvate kinase.

The flux through the glycolytic pathway is adjusted in response to conditions both inside and outside the cell. The rate in liver is regulated to meet major cellular needs:

1. the production of ATP;
2. the provision of building blocks for biosynthetic reactions; and
3. to lower blood glucose, one of the major functions of the liver.

When blood sugar falls, glycolysis is halted in liver to allow the reverse process, gluconeogenesis. In glycolysis, the reactions catalyzed by hexokinase, phosphofructokinase, and pyruvate kinase are effectively irreversible in most organisms. In metabolic pathways, such enzymes are potential sites of control, and all three enzymes serve this purpose in glycolysis.

Hexokinase

In animals, regulation of blood glucose levels by the liver is a vital part of homeostasis. In liver cells, extra G6P may be converted to G1P for conversion to glycogen, or it is alternatively converted by glycolysis to acetyl-CoA and then citrate. Excess citrate is exported to the cytosol, where ATP citrate lyase will regenerate acetyl-CoA and OAA. The acetyl-CoA is then used for fatty acid and cholesterol synthesis, two important ways of utilizing excess glucose when its concentration is high in blood. Liver contains both hexokinase and glucokinase; the latter catalyses the phosphorylation of glucose to G6P and is not inhibited by G6P. Thus it allows glucose to be converted into glycogen, fatty acids, and cholesterol even when hexokinase activity is low This is important when blood glucose levels are high. During hypoglycemia, the glycogen can be converted back to G6P and then converted to glucose by a liver-specific enzyme glucose 6-phosphatase. This reverse reaction is an important role of liver cells to maintain blood sugars levels during fasting. This is critical for brain function, since the brain utilizes glucose as an energy source under most conditions.

Phosphofructokinase

Phosphofructokinase is an important control point in the glycolytic pathway, since it is one of the irreversible steps and has key allosteric effectors, AMP and fructose 1,6-bisphosphate (F1,6BP).

Fructose 2,6-bisphosphate (F2,6BP) is a very potent activator of phosphofructokinase (PFK-1) that is synthesised when F6P is phosphorylated by a second phosphofructokinase (PFK2). In liver, when blood sugar is low and glucagon elevates cAMP, PFK2 is phosphorylated by protein kinase A. The phosphorylation inactivates PFK2, and another domain on this protein becomes active as fructose 2, 6-bisphosphatase, which converts F2,6BP back to F6P. Both glucagon and epinephrine cause high levels of cAMP in the liver. The result of lower levels of liver fructose-2,6-bisphosphate is a decrease in activity of phosphofructokinase and an increase in activity of fructose 1,6-bisphosphatase, so that gluconeogenesis (essentially "glycolysis in reverse") is favored. This is consistent with the role of the liver in such situations, since the response of the liver to these hormones is to release glucose to the blood.

ATP competes with AMP for the allosteric effector site on the PFK enzyme. ATP concentrations in cells are much higher than AMP, typically 100-fold higher, but the concentration of ATP does not change more than about 10% under physiological conditions, whereas a 10% drop in ATP results in a 6-fold increase in AMP Thus, the relevance of ATP as an allosteric effector is questionable. An increase in AMP is a consequence of a decrease in energy charge in the cell.

Citrate inhibits phosphofructokinase when tested *in vitro* by enhancing the inhibitory effect of ATP. However, it is doubtful that this is a meaningful effect *in vivo*, because citrate in the cytosol is mainly utilized for conversion to acetyl-CoA for fatty acid and cholesterol synthesis.

Pyruvate Kinase

This enzyme catalyzes the last step of glycolysis, in which pyruvate and ATP are formed. Regulation of this enzyme is discussed in the main topic, pyruvate kinase.

POST-GLYCOLYSIS PROCESSES

The overall process of glycolysis is:

$$\text{glucose} + 2\ NAD^+ + 2\ ADP + 2\ P_i \rightarrow 2\ \text{pyruvate} + 2\ NADH + 2\ H^+ + 2\ ATP + 2\ H_2O$$

If glycolysis were to continue indefinitely, all of the NAD+ would be used up, and glycolysis would stop. To allow glycolysis to continue, organisms must be able to oxidize NADH back to NAD^+.

Anaerobic Respiration

One method of doing this is to simply have the pyruvate do the oxidation; in this process the pyruvate is converted to lactate (the anion of lactic acid) in a process called lactic acid fermentation:

$$\text{pyruvate} + NADH + H^+ \rightarrow \text{lactate} + NAD^+$$

This process occurs in the bacteria involved in making yogurt (the lactic acid causes the milk to curdle). This process also occurs in animals under hypoxic (or partially-anaerobic) conditions, found, for example, in overworked muscles that are starved of oxygen, or in infarcted heart muscle cells. In many tissues, this is a cellular last resort for energy; most animal tissue cannot maintain anaerobic respiration for an extended length of time.

Some organisms, such as yeast, convert NADH back to NAD+ in a process called ethanol fermentation. In this process the pyruvate is converted first to acetaldehyde and carbon dioxide, then to ethanol.

Lactic acid fermentation and ethanol fermentation can occur in the absence of oxygen. This anaerobic fermentation allows many single-celled organisms to use glycolysis as their only energy source.

In the above two examples of fermentation, NADH is oxidized by transferring two electrons to pyruvate. However, anaerobic bacteria use a wide variety of compounds as the terminal electron acceptors in cellular respiration: nitrogenous compounds, such as nitrates and nitrites; sulfur compounds, such as sulfates, sulfites, sulfur dioxide, and elemental sulfur; carbon dioxide; iron compounds; manganese compounds; cobalt compounds; and uranium compounds.

Aerobic Respiration

In aerobic organisms, a complex mechanism has evolved to use the oxygen in air as the final electron acceptor of respiration.

- First, pyruvate is converted to acetyl-CoA and CO_2 within the mitochondria in a process called pyruvate decarboxylation.
- Second, the acetyl-CoA enters the citric acid cycle, where it is fully oxidized to carbon dioxide and water, producing yet more NADH.

- Third, the NADH is oxidized to NAD+ by the electron transport chain, using oxygen as the final electron acceptor. This process creates a "hydrogen ion gradient" across the inner membrane of the mitochondria.
- Fourth, the proton gradient is used to produce a large amount of ATP in a process called oxidative phosphorylation.

Intermediates for Other Pathways

This article concentrates on the catabolic role of glycolysis with regard to converting potential chemical energy to usable chemical energy during the oxidation of glucose to pyruvate. However, many of the metabolites in the glycolytic pathway are also used by anabolic pathways, and, as a consequence, flux through the pathway is critical to maintain a supply of carbon skeletons for biosynthesis.

In addition, not all carbon entering the pathway leaves as pyruvate and may be extracted at earlier stages to provide carbon compounds for other pathways.

These metabolic pathways are all strongly reliant on glycolysis as a source of metabolites:

- Gluconeogenesis
- Lipid metabolism
- Pentose phosphate pathway

Citric acid cycle, which in turn leads to:

- Amino acid synthesis
- Nucleotide synthesis
- Tetrapyrrole synthesis

From an anabolic metabolism perspective, the NADH has a role to drive synthetic reactions, doing so by directly or indirectly reducing the pool of $NADP^+$ in the cell to NADPH, which is another important reducing agent for biosynthetic pathways in a cell.

GLYCOLYSIS IN DISEASES

Genetic Diseases

Glycolytic mutations are generally rare due to importance of the metabolic pathway, however some mutations are seen.

Alignant rapidly-growing tumor cells typically have glycolytic rates that are up to 200 times higher than those of their normal tissues of origin. There are two common explanations. The classical explanation is that there is poor blood supply to tumors causing local depletion of oxygen. There is also evidence that attributes some of these high aerobic glycolytic rates to an overexpressed form of mitochondrially-bound hexokinase responsible for driving the high glycolytic activity. This phenomenon was first described in 1930 by Otto Warburg, and hence it is referred to as the Warburg effect. Warburg hypothesis claims that cancer is primarily caused by dysfunctionality in mitochondrial metabolism, rather than because of uncontrolled growth of cells. There is ongoing research to affect mitochondrial metabolism and treat cancer by starving cancerous cells in various new ways, including a ketogenic diet.

CHAPTER 4

Starch

Starch, chemical formula $(C_6H_{10}O_5)_n$, (CAS 9005-25-8) is a polysaccharide carbohydrate consisting of a large number of glucose monosaccharide units joined together by glycosidic bonds. Starch is produced by plants. Through photosynthesis glucose is produced and plants store energy mainly as starch. Starch exists in two types of molecules : the linear amylose and the branched amylopectin.

Starch is a polysaccharide carbohydrate found in plant cells. It is formed from the covalent bonding of a large number of glucose monosaccharide units. The glucose is made by the plant cells and is stored as starch, ready to use for energy when it is needed. Starch consists of two molecules; amylaseamylose and amylopectin.

Starch use for Plants

Plants use starch as a way to store excess glucose, and use starch as food during mitochondrial oxidative phosphorylation. Starch is the main storage of energy for plants. Starch is all over the plant. Toward the end of the growing season starch accumulates in twigs of trees near the buds. Fruit, seeds, rhizomes, and tubers store starch to start the growth next spring.

Tests

It is thought that the iodine fits inside the coils of amylose A 0.3% w/w solution is the standard concentration for a dilute starch indicator solution. It is made by adding 4 grams of soluble starch to 1 litre of heated water; the solution is cooled before use (starch-iodine complex becomes unstable at temperatures above 35 °C). This complex is often used in redox titrations: in presence of an oxidizing agent the solution turns blue, in the presence of reducing agent, the blue color disappears because triiodide (I3-) ions break up into three iodide ions, disassembling the complex.

Microscopy of Starch Granules

Each species of plant has an unique shape of starch granules in granular size, shape and crystallisation pattern.Under the microscope, starch grains stained with iodine illuminated from behind with polarized light show a distinctive Maltese cross effect (also known as extinction cross and birefringence).

Starch, Nutrient for Humans

Starch is a main nutrient for humans. The major sources of starch intake in the human diet worldwide are rice, wheat, corn, potatoes, cassava. Well-known prepared foods based on starch roots or seeds are also bread, pancakes, cereals, noodles, pasta and tortilla. Depending on the local climate other starch sources are used as arrowroot, arracacha, buckwheat, banana, barley, kudzu, oca, sago, sorghum, sweet potato, taro and yams. Edible beans, such as favas, lentils and peas, are also rich in starch.

Note: Fresh chestnut has twice as much starch as potato. As the chestnut ripens, some of its starch is gradually converted into sugars.

Commercial Available Starch Powder

The starch industry extracts and refines starches from seeds and roots. Today, main commercial refined starches are cornstarch, tapioca, wheat and potato starch. To a lesser extent also other source are used as rice, sago and peas. Historically Florida arrowroot was also commercialized. Still more than 50 types of plants are used to make starch from.

'Amylose and amylopectine - Starch generally contains 20 to 25 per cent amylose and 75 to 80 per cent amylopectin. Depending on the plant this varies, some types of starches as waxy maize, amylopectine potato starch contain mainly amylopectine and high amylose corn starch contain much more amylose.

Native Starch

Refined starch is called native starch and used in cooking to thicken foods such as sauces and soups, making noodles, pastas. In industrial application, it is used in the manufacturing of corrugated board adhesives, paper, textiles and as a mold in the manufacture of sweets such as wine gums and jelly beans.

Modified Starch

A modified food starch undergoes one or more chemical modifications, which allow the starch for example to function properly such as under high heat, and/or shear frequently encountered during processing and conditions during storage such as cooling.

When a starch is pre-cooked, it can then be used to thicken instant in cold water. This is referred to as a pregelatinized starch. Otherwise starch requires heat to thicken, or "gelatinize". The actual temperature depends on the type of starch.

The modified starches are coded according to the International Numbering System for Food Additives (INS):

1401	Acid-treated starch
1402	Alkaline-treated starch
1403	Bleached starch
1404	Oxidized starch
1405	Starches, enzyme-treated
1410	Monostarch phosphate
1411	Distarch glycerol
1412	Distarch phosphate esterified with sodium trimetaphosphate
1413	Phosphated distarch phosphate
1414	Acetylated distarch phosphate
1420	Starch acetate esterified with acetic anhydride
1421	Starch acetate esterified with vinyl acetate
1422	Acetylated distarch adipate
1423	Acetylated distarch glycerol
1440	Hydroxypropyl starch
1442	Hydroxypropyl distarch phosphate
1443	Hydroxypropyl distarch glycerol
1450	Starch sodium octenyl succinate
1451	Acetylated oxidized starch

Some other types of modified starches commercially available are dextrins, cationic starches, carboxymethylated starches.

Starch Sugars

Starch are hydrolyzed into simpler carbohydrates by acids, various enzymes, or a combination of the two. The extent of conversion is typically quantified by dextrose equivalency (DE), which is roughly the fraction of the glycoside bonds in starch that have been broken. Food products made in this way include: Maltodextrin, a lightly hydrolyzed (DE 10–20) starch product used as a bland-tasting filler and thickener.

Various glucose syrup/corn syrups (DE 30-70), viscous solutions used as sweeteners and thickeners in many kinds of processed foods.

Dextrose (DE 100), commercial glucose, prepared by the complete hydrolysis of starch.

High fructose syrup, made by treating dextrose solutions with the enzyme glucose isomerase, until a substantial fraction of the glucose has been converted to fructose. In the United States, high fructose corn syrup is the principal sweetener used in sweetened beverages because fructose has better handling characteristics, such as microbiological stability, and more consistent sweetness/flavour. High fructose corn syrup has the same sweetness as sugar.

Food Ingredients

As an additive for food processing, food starches are typically used as thickeners and stabilizers in foods such as puddings, custards, soups, sauces, gravies, pie fillings, and salad dressings, but have many other uses. But by far most starch based food ingredient used in food is glucose and use as sweetener in many drinks and foods as partially as a substitute for beet sugar.

Use as a Mold

Gummed sweets such as jelly beans and wine gums are not manufactured using a mold in the conventional sense. A tray is filled with native starch and leveled. A positive mold is then pressed into the starch leaving an impression of 1000 or so jelly beans. The mix is then poured into the impressions and then put into a stove to set. This method greatly reduces the number of molds that must be manufactured.

Resistant starch is starch that escapes digestion in the small intestine of healthy individuals.

Industrial Applications

Starch adhesive papermaking is the largest non-food application for starches globally, consuming millions of metric tons annually. In a typical sheet of copy paper for instance, the starch content may be as high as 8%. Both chemically modified and unmodified starches are used in papermaking. In the wet part of the papermaking process, generally called the "wet-end", the starches used are cationic and have a positive charge bound to the starch polymer. These starch derivatives associate with the anionic or negatively charged paper fibres/cellulose and inorganic fillers. Cationic starches together with other retention and internal sizing agent help to give the necessary strength properties to the paper web to be formed in the papermaking process (wet strength), and to provide strength to the final paper sheet (dry strength).

In the dry end of the papermaking process the paper web is rewetted with a starch based solution. The process is called surface sizing. Starches used have been chemically, or enzymatically depolymerized at the paper mill or by the starch industry (oxidized starch). The size - starch solutions are applied to the paper web by means of various mechanical presses (size press). Together with surface sizing agent the surface starches impart additional strength to the paper web and additionally provide water hold out or "size" for superior printing properties. Starch is also used in paper coating as one of the binders for the coating formulation a mixure of pigments, binders and thickeners. Coated paper has improved smoothness, hardness, whitness and gloss and thus improves printing charateristics.

Corrugated board adhesives are the next largest application of non-food starches globally. Starch glues are mostly based on unmodified native starches plus some additive as borax and caustic soda. Part of the starch is gelatinized to carrier slurry of uncooked starches and prevent sedimentation. This opaque glue is called a SteinHall adhesives. The glue is applied on tips of the fluting. The fluted paper is pressed to paper called liner. This is then dried under high heat, which causes the rest of the uncooked starch in glue to swell/gelatinize. This gelatinizing makes the glue a fast and strong for corrugated board production.

Another large non-food starch application is in the construction industry where starch is used in the gypsum wall board manufacturing process. Chemically modified or unmodified starches are added to the stucco containing primarily gypsum. Top and bottom heavyweight sheets of paper are applied to the formulation and the process is allowed to heat and cure to form the eventual rigid wall board. The starches act as a glue for the cured gypsum rock with the paper covering and also provide rigidity to the board.

Clothing starch or laundry starch is a liquid that is prepared by mixing a vegetable starch in water (earlier preparations also had to be boiled), and is used in the laundering of clothes. Starch was widely used in Europe in the 16th and 17th centuries to stiffen the wide collars and ruffs of fine linen which surrounded the necks of the well-to-do. During the 19th century and early 20th century, it was stylish to stiffen the collars and sleeves of men's shirts and the ruffles of girls' petticoats by applying starch to them as the clean clothes were being ironed. Aside from the smooth, crisp edges it gave to clothing, it served practical purposes as well. Dirt and sweat from a person's neck and wrists would stick to the starch rather than fibers of the clothing, and would easily wash away along with the starch. After each laundering, the starch would be reapplied. Today the product is sold in aerosol cans for home use.

Starch is also used to make some packing peanuts, and some dropped ceiling tiles.

Textile Chemicals

To reduce breaking of yarns of during weaving, the warp yarns are sized. Starch is one of the main textile sizing agents used for cotton sizing. Starch is also used as printing thickener.

Adhesives

Starch is also used in the manufacture of glues for book-binding, wallpaper adhesives, paper sack production, tube winding, gummed paper, envelop adhesives, school glues, bottle labeling.

Starch derivatives as yellow dextrins can be modified by addition of some chemical forms to be a hard glue for paper work, some of those forms are Borax , Soda Ash , which mixed with the starch solution at 50-70C to gain a very good adhesive, Sodium Silicate can be added to reinforce this formula.

Printing Industry

In the printing industry food grade starch is used in the manufacture of anti-set-off spray powder used to separate printed sheets of paper to avoid wet ink being set off.

Hydrogen Production

Starch can be used to produce Hydrogen.

Bio-ethanol

Glucose is further fermented to ethanol.

Oil Exploration

starch is used as to adjust the viscosity of drilling fluid which is used to lubricate the drill head in (mineral) oil extraction.

Body Powder

Powdered corn starch is used as a substitute for talcum powder in many health and beauty products.

Excipient

Starch is used as binder in medications to aid the formation of tablets.

Modified Starch

Modified starch is a food additive which is prepared by treating starch or starch granules, causing the starch to be partially degraded. Modified starch is used as a thickening agent, stabilizer, or an emulsifier. Apart from food products, modified starch is also found in pharmaceuticals.

Starches are modified for a number of reasons. Starches may be modified to increase their stability against excessive heat, acid, and freezing; to change their texture; or to lengthen or shorten gelatinization time.

A modified starch may be an instant starch which thickens and gels without heat; or a cook-up starch, such as Colflo 67, which must be cooked like regular starch.

Acid-treated starch (E1401), usually simply called "modified starch", is prepared by treating starch or starch granules with inorganic acids.

Other treatments may produce modified starch with different E numbers, such as alkaline-modified starch (E1402), bleached starch (E1403), oxidized starch (E1404), enzyme-treated starch (INS: 1405), acetylated starch (E1420), and acetylated oxidized starch (E1451).

Pre-gelatinized starch is used to thicken instant desserts, allowing the food to thicken with the addition of cold water or milk. Similarly, cheese sauce granules (such as in Macaroni and Cheese or lasagna) or gravy granules may be thickened with boiling water without the product going lumpy. Commercial pizza toppings containing modified starch will thicken when heated in the oven, keeping them on top of the pizza, and then become runny when cooled.

A suitably-modified starch is used, quite successfully (with respect to the taste), as a fat substitute for low-fat versions of traditionally fatty foods, e.g., reduced-fat hard salami having about 1/3rd the usual fat content. For such uses, it is an alternative to the product Olestra.

Modified starch is added to frozen products to prevent them from dripping when defrosted. Modified starch, bonded with phosphate, allows the starch to absorb more water and keeps the ingredients together. Modified starch acts as an emulsifier for French dressing by enveloping oil droplets and suspending them in the water. Acid-treated starch forms the shell of jelly beans. Oxidized starch increases the stickiness of batter.

Genetically Modified Starch

Modified starch should not be confused with genetically modified starch, which refers to starch from genetically engineered plants, which have been genetically modified to produce novel carbohydrates which might not naturally occur in the plant species being harvested. The modification in this sense refers to the genetic engineering of the plant DNA, and not the later processing or treatment of the starch or starch granules.

Genetically modified starch is of interest in the manufacture of biodegradable polymers and noncellulose feedstock in the paper industry, as well as the creation of new food additives.

CHAPTER

5

Lipid

Lipids are broadly defined as any fat-soluble (lipophilic), naturally-occurring molecule, such as fats, oils, waxes, cholesterol, sterols, fat-soluble vitamins (such as vitamins A, D, E and K), monoglycerides, diglycerides, phospholipids, and others. The main biological functions of lipids include energy storage, acting as structural components of cell membranes, and participating as important signaling molecules.

Although the term lipid is sometimes used as a synonym for fats, fats are a subgroup of lipids called triglycerides and should not be confused with the term fatty acid. Lipids also encompass molecules such as fatty acids and their derivatives (including tri-, di-, and monoglycerides and phospholipids), as well as other sterol-containing metabolites such as cholesterol. The emulsion test is a crude method for determining the presence or absence of lipids in a given sample.

Lipids are a diverse group of compounds that have many key biological functions, such as structural components of cell membranes, energy storage sources and intermediates in signaling pathways. Lipids may be broadly defined as hydrophobic or amphiphilic small molecules that originate entirely or in part from two distinct types of biochemical subunits or "building blocks": ketoacyl and isoprene groups. Using this approach, lipids may be divided into eight categories : fatty acyls, glycerolipids, glycerophospholipids, sphingolipids, saccharo-lipids and polyketides (derived from condensation of ketoacyl subunits); and sterol lipids and prenol lipids (derived from condensation of isoprene.

CATEGORIES OF LIPIDS

Fatty Acyls

Fatty acyls (including fatty acids) are a diverse group of molecules synthesized by chain-elongation of an acetyl-CoA primer with malonyl-CoA or methylmalonyl-CoA groups. The fatty acyl structure represents the major lipid building block of complex lipids and therefore is one of the most fundamental categories of biological lipids. The carbon chain may be saturated or unsaturated, and may be attached to functional groups containing oxygen, halogens, nitrogen and sulfur. Examples of biologically interesting fatty acyls are the eicosanoids which are in turn derived from arachidonic acid which include prostaglandins, leukotrienes, and thromboxanes. Other major lipid classes in the fatty acyl category are the fatty esters and fatty amides. Fatty esters include important biochemical intermediates such as wax esters, fatty acyl thioester coenzyme A derivatives, fatty acyl thioester ACP derivatives and fatty acyl carnitines. The fatty amides include N-acyl ethanolamines such as anandamide.

Glycerolipids

Glycerolipids are composed mainly of mono-, di- and tri-substituted glycerols the most well-known being the fatty acid esters of glycerol (triacylglycerols), also known as triglycerides. these comprise the bulk of storage fat in animal tissues. Additional subclasses are represented by glycosylglycerols, which are characterized by the presence of one or more sugar residues attached to glycerol via a glycosidic linkage. Examples of structures in this category are the digalactosyldiacylglycerols found in plant membranes and seminolipid from mammalian spermatazoa.

Glycerophospholipids

Glycerophospholipids, also referred to as phospholipids, are ubiquitous in nature and are key components of the lipid bilayer of cells, as well as being involved in metabolism and signaling. Glycerophospholipids may be subdivided into distinct classes, based on the nature of the polar headgroup at the *sn-3* position of the glycerol backbone in eukaryotes and eubacteria or the *sn-1* position in the case of archaebacteria. Examples of glycerophospholipids found in biological membranes are phosphatidylcholine (also known as PC or GPCho, and lecithin), phosphatidylethanolamine (PE or GPEtn) and phosphati-dylserine (PS or GPSer). In addition to serving as a primary component of cellular membranes and binding sites for intra- and intercellular proteins, some glycerophospholipids in eukaryotic cells, such as phosphatidylinositols and phosphatidic acids are either precursors of, or are themselves, membrane-derived second messengers. Typically one or both of these hydroxyl groups are acylated with long-chain fatty acids, but there are also alkyl-linked and 1Z-alkenyl-linked (plasmalogen) glyceropho-spholipids, as well as dialkylether variants in prokaryotes.

Sphingolipids

Sphingolipids are a complex family of compounds that share a common structural feature, a sphingoid base backbone that is synthesized *de novo* from serine and a long-chain fatty acyl CoA, then converted into ceramides, phosphosphingolipids, glycosphingolipids and other species.

The major sphingoid base of mammals is commonly referred to as sphingosine. Ceramides (N-acyl-sphingoid bases) are a major subclass of sphingoid base derivatives with an amide-linked fatty acid. The fatty acids are typically saturated or mono-unsaturated with chain lengths from 14 to 26 carbon atoms. The major phosphosphingolipids of mammals are sphingomyelins (ceramide phosphocholines), whereas insects contain mainly ceramide phosphoethanolamines and fungi have phytoceramide-phosphoinositols and mannose containing headgroups. The Glycosphingolipids are a diverse family of molecules composed of one or more sugar residues linked via a glycosidic bond to the sphingoid base. Examples of these are the simple and complex glycosphingolipids such as cerebrosides and gangliosides.

Sterol Lipids

Sterol lipids, such as cholesterol and its derivatives are an important component of membrane lipids along with the glycerophospholipids and sphingomyelins. The steroids, which also contain the same fused four-ring core structure, have different biological roles as hormones and signaling molecules. The C18 steroids include the estrogen family whereas the C19 steroids comprise the androgens such as testosterone and androsterone. The C21 subclass includes the progestogens as well as the glucocorticoids and mineralocorticoids. The secosteroids, comprising various forms of vitamin D, are characterized by cleavage of the B ring of the core structure. Other examples of sterols are the bile acids and their conjugates, which in mammals are oxidized derivatives of cholesterol and are synthesized in the liver.

Prenol Lipids

Prenol lipids are synthesized from the 5-carbon precursors isopentenyl diphosphate and dimethylallyl diphosphate that are produced mainly via the mevalonic acid

(MVA) pathway. The simple isoprenoids (linear alcohols, diphosphates, etc.) are formed by the successive addition of C5 units, and are classified according to number of these terpene units. Structures containing greater than 40 carbons are known as polyterpenes. Carotenoids are important simple isoprenoids that function as anti-oxidants and as precursors of vitamin A. Another biologically important class of molecules is exemplified by the quinones and hydroquinones, which contain an isoprenoid tail attached to a quinonoid core of non-isoprenoid origin. Vitamin E and vitamin K, as well as the ubiquinones, are examples of this class. Bacteria synthesize polyprenols (called bactoprenols) in which the terminal isoprenoid unit attached to oxygen remains unsaturated, whereas in animal polyprenols (dolichols) the terminal isoprenoid is reduced.

Saccharolipids

Saccharolipids describe compounds in which fatty acids are linked directly to a sugar backbone, forming structures that are compatible with membrane bilayers. In the saccharolipids, a sugar substitutes for the glycerol backbone that is present in glycerolipids and glycero-phospholipids. The most familiar saccharolipids are the acylated glucosamine precursors of the Lipid A component of the lipopoly-saccharides in Gram-negative bacteria. Typical lipid A molecules are disaccharides of glucosamine, which are derivatized with as many as seven fatty-acyl chains. The minimal lipopolysaccharide required for growth in E. coli is Kdo2-Lipid A, a hexa-acylated disaccharide of glucosamine that is glycosylated with two 3-deoxy-D-manno-octulosonic acid (Kdo) residues.

Polyketides

Polyketides are synthesized by polymerization of acetyl and propionyl subunits by classic enzymes as well as iterative and multimodular enzymes that share mechanistic features with the fatty acid synthases. They comprise a very large number of secondary metabolites and natural products from animal, plant, bacterial, fungal and marine sources, and have great structural diversity. Many polyketides are cyclic molecules whose backbones are often further modified by glycosylation, methylation, hydroxylation, oxidation, and/or other processes. Many commonly used anti-microbial, anti-parasitic, and anti-cancer agents are polyketides or polyketide derivatives, such as erythromycins, tetracylines, avermectins, and antitumor epothilones.

Biological Functions

Membranes

All eukaryotic cells are compartmentalized into membrane-bound organelles which carry out different functions. These glycerophospholipids are amphipathic molecules that contain a glycerol core linked to two fatty acid-derived "tails" by ester or, more rarely, ether linkages and to one "head" group by a phosphate ester linkage. While glycerophospholipids are the major component of biological membranes, other non-glyceride lipid components such as sphingomyelin and sterols (mainly cholesterol in animal cell membranes) are also found in biological membranes. In plants and algae, the galactosyldiacylglycerols, and sulfoquinovosyldiacylglycerol which lack a phosphate group, are important components of membranes of chloroplasts and related organelles and are the most abundant lipids in photosynthetic tissues, including those of higher plants, algae and certain bacteria.

A biological membrane is a form of lipid bilayer, as is a liposome. The formation of lipid bilayers is an energetically-preferred process when the glycero-phospholipids described above are in an aqueous environment. In an aqueous system, the polar heads of lipids orientate towards the polar, aqueous environment, while the hydrophobic tails minimise their contact with water. The lipophilic tails of lipids (U) tend to cluster together, forming a lipid bilayer (1) or a micelle (2). Other aggregations are also observed and form part of the polymorphism of amphiphile (lipid) behaviour. The polar heads (P) face the aqueous environment, curving away from the water. Phase behaviour is a complicated area within biophysics and is the subject of current academic research. Micelles and bilayers form in the polar medium by a process known as the hydrophobic effect When dissolving a lipophilic or amphiphilic substance in a polar environment, the polar molecules (i.e. water in an aqueous solution) become more ordered around the dissolved lipophilic substance, since the polar molecules cannot form hydrogen bonds to the lipophilic areas of the amphiphile. So in an aqueous environment the water molecules form an ordered "clathrate" cage around the dissolved lipophilic molecule.

Energy Storage and Metabolism

Triacylglycerols, stored in adipose tissue, are a major form of energy storage in animals. Animals use triglycerides for energy storage because of its high caloric content (9.4 kcal/g), whereas plants, which do not require energy for movement, can afford to store food for energy in a less compact but more easily accessible form, such as starch (carbohydrate). Triglycerides and phospholipids are broken down into free fatty acids by the action of lipases. Beta oxidation is the process by which fatty acids, in the form of acyl-CoA molecules, are broken down in the mitochondria and/or in peroxisomes to generate acetyl-CoA. The acetyl CoA is then ultimately converted into ATP, CO_2, and H_2O using the citric acid cycle and the electron transport chain. Conversely, fatty acid biosynthesis (Lipogenesis) takes place in the cytoplasm, using acetyl-CoA (derived from carbohydrates, amino acids or fatty acids) as the precursor. The fatty acids may be subsequently converted to triacylglycerols that are packaged in lipoproteins (VLDL's) and secreted from the liver.

Signalling

Lipid signalling may occur via activation of G-protein-coupled or nuclear receptors, and members of several different lipid categories have been identified as signaling molecules and cellular messengers These include sphingosine-1-phosphate, a sphingolipid derived from ceramide that is a potent messenger molecule involved in regulating calcium mobilization, cell growth, apoptosis; diacylglycerol (DAG) and the phosphatidylinositol phosphates (PIPs), involved in calcium-mediated activation of protein kinase C; the prostaglandins, arachidonic acid -derived fatty acids involved in inflammation and immunity; the steroid hormones such as estrogen, testosterone and cortisol, which modulate a host of functions such as reproduction, metabolism and blood pressure; and the oxysterols such as 25-hydroxy-cholesterol that are Liver X receptor (LXR) agonists.

Other Functions

The "fat-soluble" vitamins (A, D, E and K) which are isoprene-based lipids are essential nutrients stored in the liver and fatty tissues. These have a diverse range of functions discussed elsewhere. Acyl-carnitines are involved in the transport and metabolism of fatty acids in and out of mitochondria, where they undergo beta oxidation. Polyprenols and their phosphorylated derivatives also play important transport roles, in this case the transport of oligosaccharides across membranes. Polyprenol phosphate sugars and polyprenol diphosphate sugars function in extra-cytoplasmic glycosylation reactions, in extra-cellular polysaccharide biosynthesis (for instance peptidoglycan polymerization in bacteria), and in eukaryotic protein N-glycosylation. Cardiolipins are a subclass of glycerophospholipids containing four acyl chains and three glycerol groups that are particularly abundant in the inner mitochondrial membrane. They are believed to activate enzymes involved with oxidative phosphorylation.

Nutrition and Health

Lipids play diverse and important roles in nutrition and health Many lipids are absolutely essential for life. However, there is also considerable awareness that abnormal levels of certain lipids, particularly cholesterol (in hypercholesterolemia) and trans fatty acids, are risk factors for heart disease amongst others.

Humans have a requirement for certain essential fatty acids, such as linoleic acid (an omega-6 fatty acid) and alpha-linolenic acid (an omega-3 fatty acid) in the diet because they cannot be synthesized from simple precursors in the diet. Both of these fatty acids are 18-carbon polyunsaturated fatty acids differing in the number and position of the double bonds. Most vegetable oils are rich in linoleic acid (safflower, sunflower, and corn oils). Alpha-linolenic acid is found in the green leaves of plants, and in selected seeds, nuts and legumes (flax, canola, walnuts and soy). Fish oils are particularly rich in the longer-chain omega-3 fatty acids eicosapentaenoic acid (EPA) and docosahexaenoic acid (DHA). Most of the lipid found in food is in the form of triacylglycerols, cholesterol and phospholipids.

Most of the saturated fatty acids (as triacylglycerols) in the diet are incorporated into adipose tissue stores, because the absence of double bonds allows a higher energy yield per carbon than is obtained from oxidation of unsaturated fatty acids. The longer chain fatty acids are incorporated into cell membranes as phospholipids regardless of degree of saturation. Since dietary fatty acids are exchanged with membrane fatty acids, dietary fat composition is reflected in membrane lipid composition. Thus dietary fatty acids can influence cell function through effects on membrane properties. Dietary fat provides an average energy intake which is approximately twice that of carbohydrate or protein. A minimum amount of dietary fat is necessary to facilitate absorption of fat-soluble vitamins (A, D, E and K) and carotenoids. A minimal amount of body fat is also necessary to provide insulation that prevents heat loss and protects vital organs from shock due to ordinary activities.

High fat intake contributes to increased risk of obesity diabetes and atherosclerosis Atherosclerosis is the primary cause of coronary and cardiovascular diseases and is primary due to the buildup of plaque on the inside walls of arteries. ns (LDL), macrophages, smooth muscle cells, platelets, and other substances. In North America and most other western countries, atherosclerosis is the leading cause of illness and death, almost doubling the number of deaths from cancers Despi osclerotic stroke are responsible for more deaths than all other causes combined. A substantial amount of scientific evidence supports the impact of dietary fatty acids on cardiovascular health Saturated fats have a profound hypercholesterolemic (increase blood cholesterol levels) effec and tend to increase plasma LDL They are found predominantly in animal products (butter, cheese and meat) but coconut oil and palm oil are common vegetable sources. Intake of monounsaturated fats in oils such as olive oil is thought to be preferable to consumption of polyunsaturated fats in oils such as corn oil because the monounsaturated fats apparently do not lower high-density-lipoprotein (HDL) cholesterol levels Keeping cholesterol in the normal range not only helps prevent heart attacks and strokes but may also prevent the progression of atherosclerosis. "Statins" are a class of drugs that lowers the level of cholesterol in the blood by inhibiting HMG-CoA reductase which is a key enzyme involved in the biosynthesis of cholesterol in the liver.

ACTIVATORS OF G-PROTEIN COUPLED RECEPTORS

Lysophosphatidic acid (LPA)

LPA is the result of phospholipase A2 action on phosphatidic acid. The SN-1 position can contain either an ester bond or an ether bond, with ether LPA being found at elevated levels in certain cancers. LPA binds the high-affinity G-protein coupled receptors LPA1, LPA2, and LPA3 (also known as EDG2, EDG4, and EDG7, respectively).

Sphingosine-1-phosphate (S1P)

S1P is present at high concentrations in plasma and secreted locally at elevated concentrations at sites of inflammation. It is formed by the regulated phosphorylation of sphingosine. It acts through five dedicated high-affinity G-protein coupled receptors, S1P1 - S1P5. Interestingly, targeted deletion of S1P1 results in lethality in mice and deletion of S1P2 results in seizures and deafness. Additionally, a mere 3- to 5-fold elevation in serum S1P concentrations induces sudden cardiac death by an S1P3-receptor specific mechanism.

Platelet Activating Factor (PAF)

PAF is a potent activator of platelet aggregation, inflammation, and anaphylaxis. It is similar to the ubiquitous membrane phospholipid phosphatidylcholine except that it contains an acetyl-group in the SN-2 position and the SN-1 position contains an ether-linkage. PAF signals through a dedicated G-protein coupled receptor, PAFR and is inactivated by PAF acetylhydrolase.

The Endocannabinoids

The endogenous cannabinoids, or endocannabinoids, are endogenous lipids that activate cannabinoid receptors. The first such lipid to be isolated was anandamide which is the arachidonoyl amide of ethanolamine. Anandamide is formed via enzymatic release from N-arachidonoyl phosphatidylethanolamine by enzymes which have not yet been delineated. It activates both the CB1 receptor, found primarily in the central nervous system, and the CB2 receptor which is found primarily in lymphocytes and the periphery. It is found at very low levels (nM) in most tissues and is inactivated by the fatty acid amide hydrolase.

Subsequently, another endocannabinoid was isolated, 2-arachidonoylglycerol, which is produced when phospholipase C releases diacylglycerol which is then converted to 2-AG by diacylglycerol lipase. 2-AG can also activate both cannabinoid receptors and is inactivated by monoacylglycerol lipase. It is present at approximately 100-times the concentration of anandamide in most tissues.

Elevations in either of these lipids causes analgesia and anti-inflammation but the precise roles played by these two endocannabinoids are still vague and intensive research into their function, metabolism, and regulation is ongoing.

Prostaglandins

Prostaglandins are formed through oxidation of arachidonic acid by cyclooxygenases and other prostaglandin synthases. There are currently nine known G-protein coupled receptors (eicosanoid receptors) that largely mediate prostaglandin physiology.

Retinoic Acid Derivatives

Retinaldehyde is a retinoic acid derivative responsible for vision. It binds rhodopsin, a well-characterized GPCR that binds all-cis retinal in its inactive state. Upon photoisomerization by a photon the cis-retinal is converted to trans-retinal causing activation of rhodopsin which ultimately leads to depolarization of the neuron thereby enabling visual perception.

ACTIVATORS OF NUCLEAR RECEPTORS

Steroid Hormones

This large and diverse class of steroids are biosynthesized from isoprenoids and structurally resemble cholesterol. Mammalian steroid hormones can be grouped into five groups by the receptors to which they bind: glucocorticoids, mineralocorticoids, androgens, estrogens, and progestagens.

Retinoic Acid Derivatives

A number of retinol (vitamin A) derivatives activate nuclear receptors such as the RAR and RXR to mediate differentiation and proliferation of many types of cells.

Prostaglandins

The majority of prostaglandin signaling occurs via GPCRs although certain prostaglandins activate nuclear receptors in the PPAR family.

Diacylglycerol

The key event of diacylglycerol (DAG) signaling is the hydrolysis of Phosphatidylinositol (4, 5)-bisphosphate(PIP2) to DAG and inositol triphosphate (IP3) by a phospholipase C (PLC) enzyme. All six known families of PLC catalyze this reaction. IP3 is soluble and diffuses freely into the cytoplasm. It is recognised by the inositol triphosphate receptor(IP3R), a Ca^{2+} channel in the endoplasmic reticulum(ER) membrane. The ER acts as intracellular Ca^{2+} store. The binding of IP3 to IP3R releases the flow of calcium from the ER into the normally Ca^{2+}-poor cytoplasm, which then triggers various events of calcium signaling. DAG remains bound to the membrane by its fatty acid "tails" where it recruits and activates both conventional and novel members of the Protein kinase C family. Thus, both IP3 and DAG contribute to activation of PKCs.

Protein kinase C-a is a conventional PKC and requires both DAG and Ca^{2+} for activity. One of the targets activated by PKC-a is phospholipase D, which hydrolyses phosphatidylcholine(PC) to choline and phosphatidic acid. The latter is rapidly converted to DAG. PC-derived DAG can be distinguished from PIP2-derived as their differ in their fatty acid composition. PC forms the bulk of the lipids of the plasma membrane and provides an inexhaustible supply of substrates for PLD. DAG produced through this mechanism may continue to activate PKC hours after the initial extracellular stimulus.

Mechanisms of Lipid Oxidative Fragmentation

Many different mechanisms have been suggested for the oxidative lipid fragmentations that produce biologically active aldehydes such as 4-hydroxynon-2-enal (HNE), oxononanoyl phosphatidylcholine (ON-PC) from linoleic acid (LA) esters, or HNE and oxovaleroyl phosphatidylcholine (OV-PC). The major goals of our research on oxidative lipid fragmentation is to conduct experiments that can distinguish between and test the operation of these various postulated mechanisms, and to determine the influence of factors such as metal ions and pH on the relative importance of competing pathways. Experimental evidence supporting or refuting the operation of one or more of the postulated mechanisms is sorely lacking. In view of the important biological activities that have already been demonstrated for such aldehydes, it is important to know the mechanisms of their formation. Some of these postulated mechanisms involve steps that are unlikely. One of those, the Esterbauer Dioxetane Mechanism, involves the fragmentation of an intermediate dioxetane (1). However, no mechanism is suggested for generating a dioxetane (presumably singlet oxygen cycloadds to the C=C bond). It seems unlikely that a 13-alkoxyl radical would be converted to the corresponding dioxetane in view of the short lifetime expected for the former. A more likely scenario would be for the 13-alkoxyl radical to abstract H first and then the resulting 13-hydroxyoctadienoate might be converted into a dioxetane. Furthermore, alternative routes are possible for generating Esterbauer's dioxetane intermediates (vide infra).

Pryor and Porter postulated several alternative mechanisms (2) that were inspired by the observation that the formation of HNE can be catalyzed by iron which

Esterbauer Dioxetane Mechanism

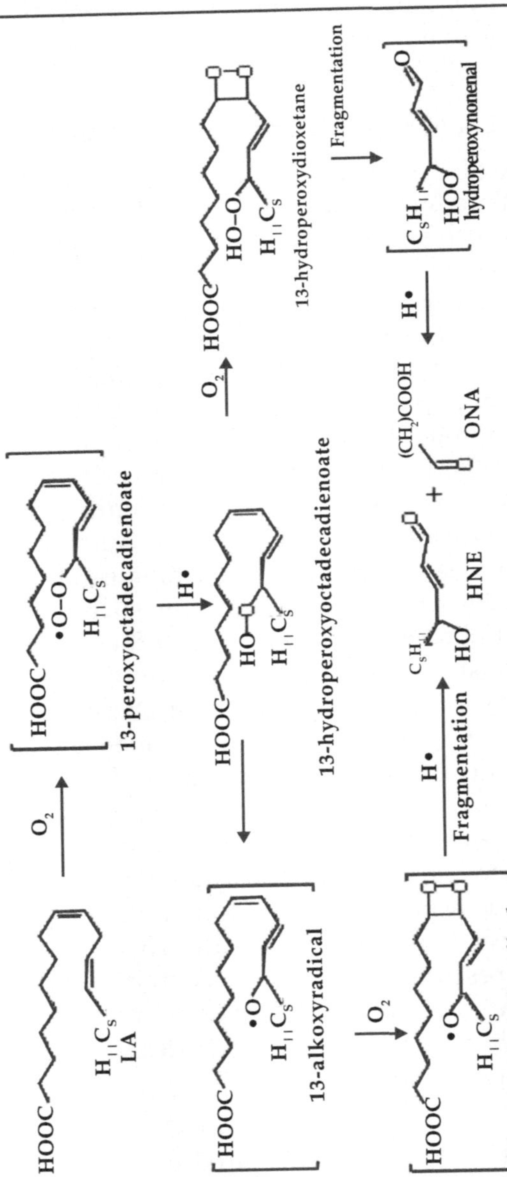

Fig. 5.1

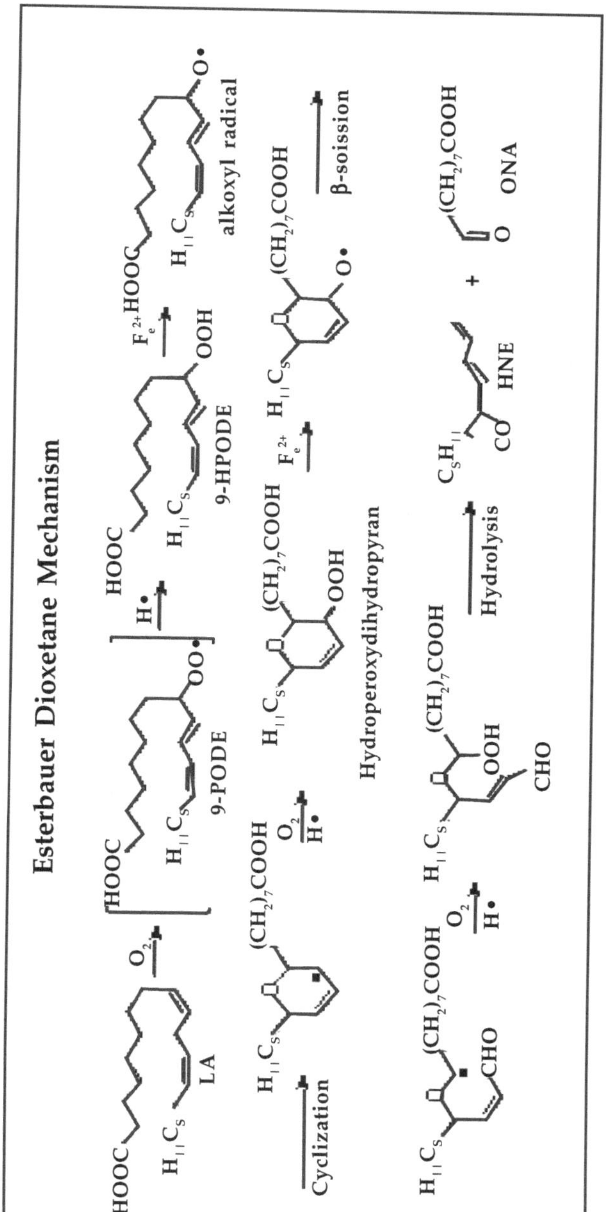
Esterbauer Dioxetane Mechanism
LA
9-PODE
9-HPODE
alkoxyl radical
Cyclization
Hydroperoxydihydropyran
β-soission
Hydrolysis
HNE
ONA

Fig. 5.2

"suggests the intermediacy of a hydroperoxide which is reduced to form an alkoxyl radical." An unlikely possibility involves the generation of a hydroperoxy dihydropyran intermediate. One difficulty with this mechanism is the geometric constraint of the C=C bonds in the alkoxyl radical intermediate which clearly would strongly disfavor cyclization.

A more reasonable scenario postulated by Pryor and Porter, involves an Epoxy Hydroperoxide Fragmentation (2). The key cyclization of an allylic alkoxyl radical to a carbon-centered allylic radical had been detected earlier (3) and has subsequently been recognized as a "key step in hydroperoxide-amplified lipid peroxidation (4). The 12,13-epoxy-9-hydroperoxide is a known product from the reaction of 13-HPODE and iron or hydrolysis of the methyl ester (5) which is generated during autoxidation of methyl linoleate (6). Several alternative mechanisms, both homo and heterolytic, were suggested for the conversion of this hydroperoxide into 3, 4-epoxynonanal that is known to rearrange readily to give HNE.

Yet another mechanism was proposed inspired by the detection of 10,13-dihydroxyoctadecadienoic acid (DHODA) as a product from the oxidation of LA. This Hydroxyhydroperoxide Mechanism generates HNE by beta-scission of a key hydroxyalkoxyl radical that is produced from a hydroxy hydroperoxide (Fig. 5.4). Formation of the hydroxy hydroperoxide could involve hydrogen abstraction from an intermediate 13-HODE. We note that an intramolecular H transfer is geometrically favorable (vide infra), bolstering the likelihood of such a mechanism. Besides HNE, the beta-scission also would generate a vinyl radical that delivers a vinyl peroxy radical by reaction with oxygen, and ultimately provides 9-oxononanoic acid (ONA) via ONA enol.

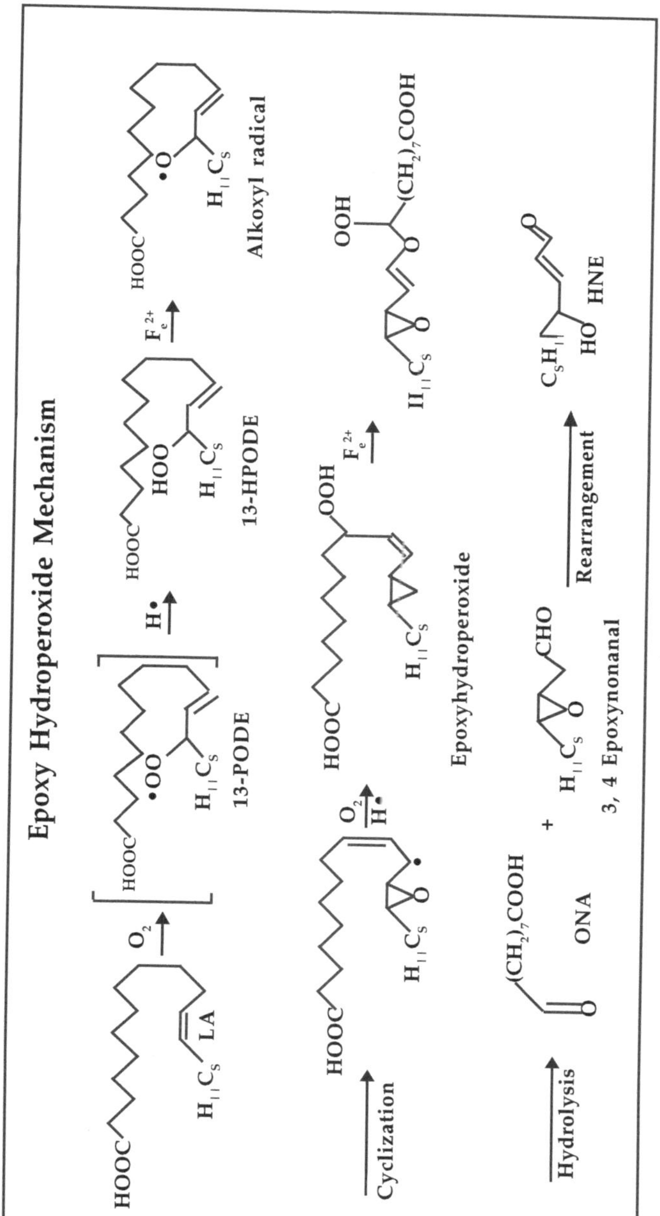
Epoxy Hydroperoxide Mechanism
LA
13-PODE
13-HPODE
Alkoxyl radical
Cyclization
Epoxyhydroperoxide
Hydrolysis
ONA
3, 4 Epoxynonanal
Rearrangement
HNE

Fig. 5.3

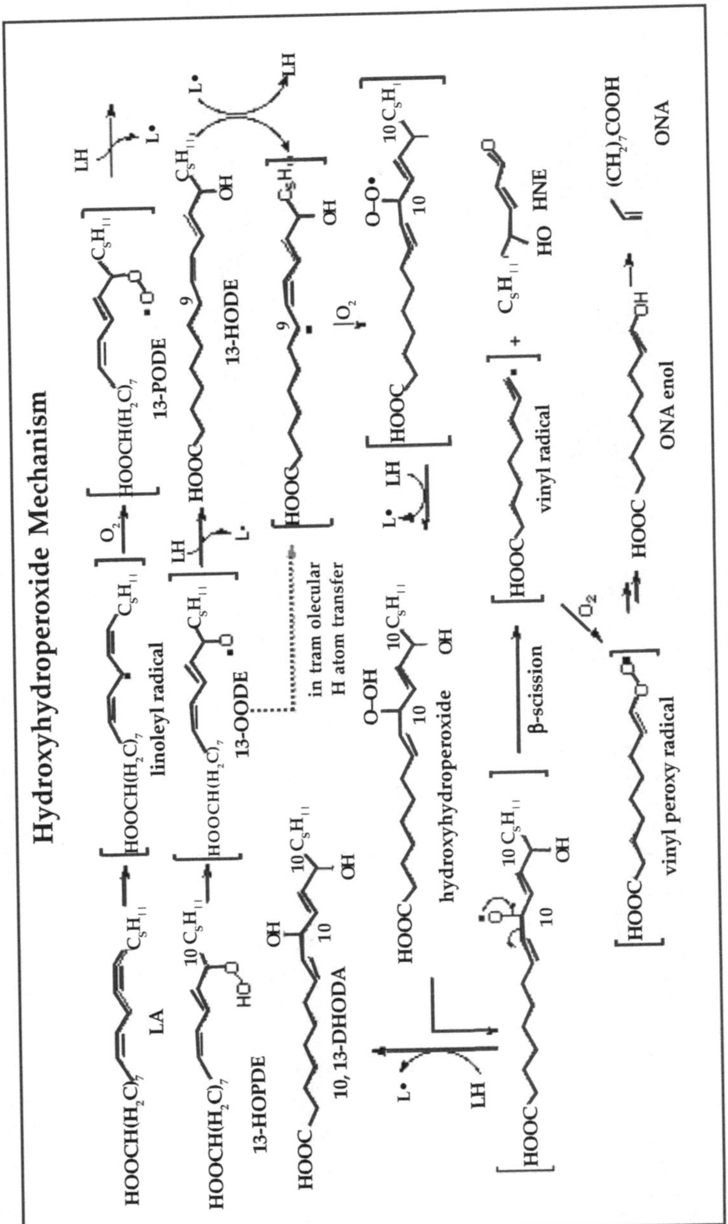
Hydroxyhydroperoxide Mechanism
LA
linoleyl radical
13-PODE
13-HOPDE
13-OODE
13-HODE
in tram olecular
H atom transfer
10, 13-DHODA
hydroxyhydroperoxide
β-scission
vinyl radical
HNE
vinyl peroxy radical
ONA enol
ONA

Fig. 5.4

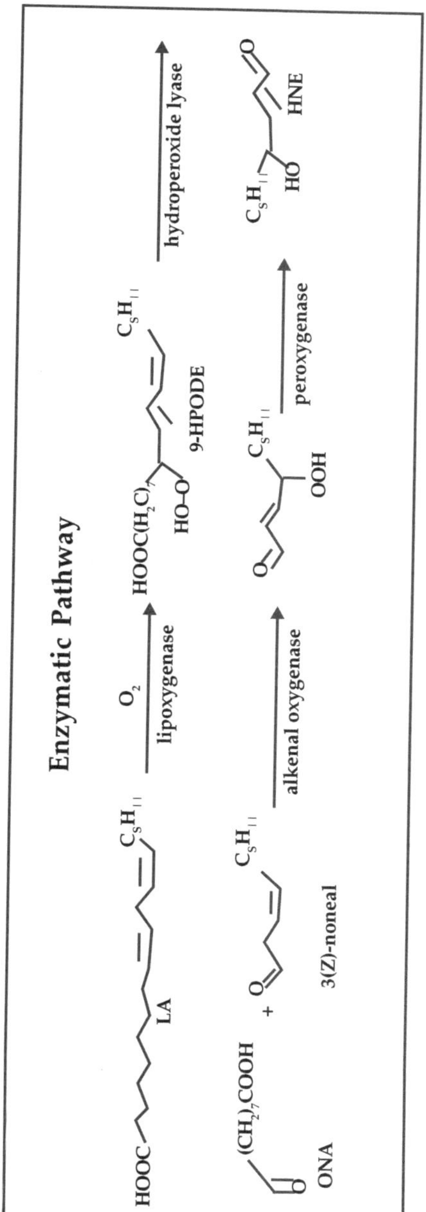
Enzymatic Pathway
HOOC
LA
C_5H_{11}
O_2
lipoxygenase
HOOC(H_2C)$_7$
HO–O
C_5H_{11}
9-HPODE
hydroperoxide lyase
O
(CH$_2$)$_7$COOH
ONA
+
O
C_5H_{11}
3(Z)-noneal
alkenal oxygenase
O
C_5H_{11}
OOH
peroxygenase
C_5H_{11}
HO
O
HNE

Fig. 5.5

Interestingly, an enzymatic route to these same products from LA was reported recently (8). Thus, 9-HPODE, generated by the action of lipoxygenase on LA, is cleaved by the action of a hydroperoxide lyase to produce ONA and 3(Z)-nonenal (Enzymatic Pathway). Alkenal oxygenase promoted oxygenation of this b,g-unsaturated aldehyde then delivers HNE.

We postulated (9) a Peroxycyclization-Dioxetane Fragmentation Mechanism (Fig. 5.6) that predicts a competition between peroxycyclization, that leads to aldehyde fragmentation products, and H transfer that produces the hydroperoxy ODAs 13-HPODE and 9-HPODE. This scenario contrasts with that envisioned in the other mechanisms proposed for HNE generation that all consider one or the other of these hydroperoxides to be intermediates leading to HNE. However, this difference between the mechanisms could easily be hidden if H transfer is readily reversible. Thus, hydroperoxides could serve as a reservoir of peroxy radicals if H abstraction from the hydroperoxy oxygen occurs readily.

Peroxycyclization of an Intermediate 5-peroxyeicosatetraenoyl radical followed by fragmentation of a dioxetane intermediate is a possible Peroxycyclization Route to OV-PC from AA-PC. The hypothetical alternative pathways outlined above illustrate the potential competition for various isomeric pentadienyl and peroxyeicosatetraenoyl radical intermediates that may be crucial for a thorough understanding of factors influencing the generation and evolution of the end products of free radical-induced lipid oxidation.

As noted above, we recently postulated a possible mechanism for oxidative fragmentation of lipids: peroxycyclization to generate a dioxetane intermediate that fragments to generate two carbonyl groups (9). Contemporaneously, this mechanism was recognized by others, and a model study was reported in which one-

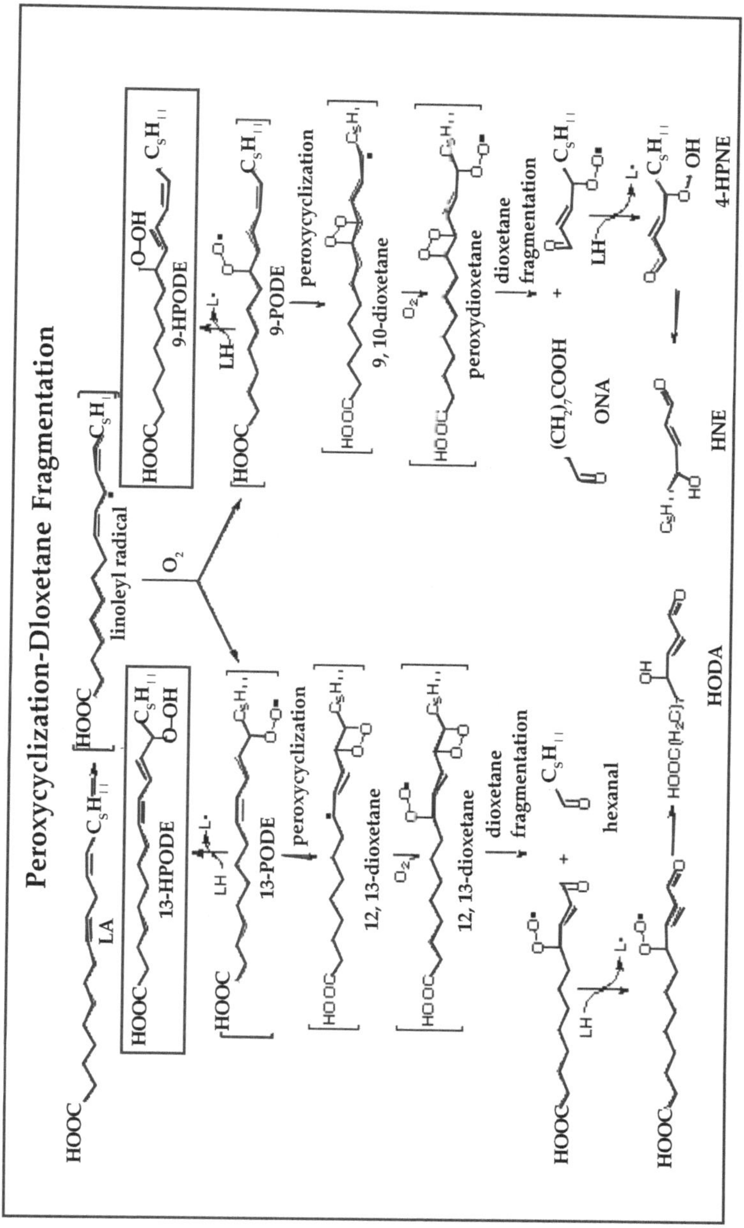
Peroxycyclization-Dloxetane Fragmentation
LA
linoleyl radical
O_2
13-HPODE
9-HPODE
13-PODE
9-PODE
peroxycyclization
peroxycyclization
12, 13-dioxetane
9, 10-dioxetane
12, 13-dioxetane
peroxydioxetane
dioxetane fragmentation
dioxetane fragmentation
hexanal
ONA
HODA
HNE
4-HPNE

Fig. 5.6

electron oxidation of an allylic hydroperoxide produces acetone and chemiluminescence, presumably by cyclization of an alkylperoxyl radical to a dioxetane radical and subsequent dioxetane fragmentation that generates triplet acetone (10). The generation of excited state carbonyl product is especially noteworthy as it is an expected consequence of orbital symmetry considerations. This observation strongly supports the involvement of a dioxetane fragmentation because there is ample precedent for this unique phenomenon.

Although the model study supports the feasibility of a peroxycyclization dioxetane-fragmentation mechanism for the formation of HNE as well as HOOA and HODA derivatives, it remains to be demonstrated that lipid peroxy radicals actually undergo such a cyclization-fragmentation. Furthermore, the simultaneous or exclusive operation of alternative mechanisms for the fragmentations which accompany free radical-induced lipid oxidations, have not been ruled out.

Lipid hydroperoxides are non-radical intermediates derived from unsaturated fatty acids, phospholipids, glycolipids, cholesterol esters and cholesterol itself. Their formation occur in enzymatic or non-enzymatic reactions involving activated chemical species known as "reactive oxygen species" (ROS) which are responsible for toxic effects in the body via various tissue damages. These ROS include among others hydroxyl radicals, lipid oxyl or peroxyl radicals, singlet oxygen, and peroxinitrite formed from nitrogen oxide (NO), all these groups of atoms behave as a unit and are now named "free radical". These chemical forms are defined as any species capable of independent existence that contains one or more unpaired electrons (those which occupy an atomic or molecular orbital by themselves). They are formed either by the loss of a single electron from a non-radical or by the gain of a single electron by a non-radical. They can easily be formed when a covalent bond is broken if one electron from each of the pair shared remains with each atom, this mechanism is known as homolytic fission. In water, this process generates the most reactive species, hydroxyl radical OH. Chemists know well that combustion which is able at high temperature to rupture C-C, C-H or C-O bonds is a free-radical process. The opposite of this mechanism is the heterolytic fission in which, after a covalent break, one atom receives both electrons while the other remains with a positive charge.

In eukaryotic organisms, ROS are mainly generated during the normal respiration process involving oxygen, oxidases and electron transports in mitochondria or endoplasmic reticulum.

Oxygen is known since a long time as poisonous as well in plants as in animals or bacteria, mainly when supplied at concentrations greater than those in normal air. Thus, oxygen is able to damage plant tissues in inhibiting chloroplast development, seed viability and root growth. The growth of bacteria (*Escherichia coli*) was shown to be slowed down by pure oxygen, the toxic effect being enhanced by ionizing radiations. Very early, it appears that the effects of oxygen and those of ionizing radiations on organisms have many similarities. In man, the toxicity of oxygen was studied in relation with diving, life in submarines and spacecrafts, treatment of some pathologies such as cancer, sclerosis or gangrene. Exposure of man to oxygen at 1 atmosphere pressure causes chest soreness, cough, sore throat, damage to lung alveoli and acute central nervous system toxicity. This toxicity was at the origin of the frequent blindness observed in the early 1940s and solved only around 1954 among infants born prematurely and kept in incubators fed with high oxygen concentrations. Several observations led Gershman R and Gilbert DL to propose in 1954, that most of the damaging effects of oxygen could be attributed to the formation of free oxygen radicals (ROS). (Gilbert DL 1981, Oxygen and living processes: an inter-disciplinary approach, Springer, NY).

History

Oxygen-dependent deterioration of lipids, known as rancidity, has been noticed since antiquity as a major problem in the storage of oils (mainly olive oil) but was also considered useful as far back as the 15th century in preparing siccative oil paints and printing inks. The same oxidation process is also considered important today for natural products used in human consumption such as fats, oils, dressings or margarine but also for chemical and industrial products such as paints, inks, resins, varnishes or lacquers.

The first studies of this lipid oxidation problem was those of the Swiss chemist Nicolas-Théodore de Saussure who observed around 1800, using a simple mercury manometer, that a layer of walnut oil exposed to air was able to absorb about 150 times its own volume of oxygen during a one year period. Parallel with these changes, oil became viscous and had a bad smell. Later, Berzelius (who discovered selenium) suggested that this oxidation might be involved in the spontaneous ignition of wool lubrified with linseed oil in textile mills. Parmentier AA, a pharmacist who introduced potato culture in France, hypothesized also that oxygen in combining with fats was the agent of rancidity.

Much information concerning the mechanism of autoxidation of lipid compounds has been obtained by the study of the oxidation of simple non fatty products such as cyclohexene. Thus, in 1928 Stephens reported the isolation of a peroxide of this compound (Stephens HN, J Am Chem Soc 1928, 50, 568). The correct structure of this peroxide was established only in 1942.

Systematic studies of lipid autoxidation may be considered to have begun around the 40s since Criegee et.al. established that hydroperoxides are the primary products of hydrocarbon oxidation. The major credit for developing the hydroperoxide hypothesis of lipid autoxidation is due to Farmer and co-workers. Bolland

(Q Rev 1949, 3, 1) established that the primary autoxidation products of linoleic acid are hydroperoxides (on carbon atom 9 or 13) containing conjugated dienes (Review in Autoxidation and antioxidants, Lundberg WO Ed, Wiley, NY 1961). Since the early 1960's, our understanding of the oxidation of unsaturated lipids has advanced considerably as a result of the application of new analytical tools. Detailed studies of the products of polyunsaturated fatty acids were initiated in the 70's by several research groups, revealing more complex mixtures than those previously proposed. With the help of HPLC, several hydroperoxide products could be separated after autoxidation of arachidonic acid (Porter NA et al., Biochem Biophys Res Comm 1979, 89, 1058), including products of lipoxygenase action. The first demonstration of free radical oxidation of membrane phospholipids was given in 1980 (Porter NA et al Lipids 1980, 15, 163) leading to a new fruitful era with a continuous flow of innumerable works devoted to chemistry, biochemistry and medicine.

CHAPTER

6

Signal Transduction

Most processes of signal transduction involve ordered sequences of biochemical reactions inside the cell, which are carried out by enzymes, activated by second messengers, resulting in a signal transduction pathway. Such processes are usually rapid, lasting on the order of milliseconds in the case of ion flux, or minutes for the activation of protein- and lipid-mediated kinase cascades, but some can take hours, and even days (as is the case with gene expression), to complete. The number of proteins and other molecules participating in the events involving signal transduction increases as the process emanates from the initial stimulus, resulting in a "signal cascade," beginning with a relatively small stimulus that elicits a large response. This is referred to as amplification of the signal.

History

Occurrence of the term "signal transduction" The total number of papers published in each year since 1977 containing the specific phrase "signal transduction" in either their title or abstract section are plotted. These figures were extracted through an analysis of the papers contained within the Medline database.The earliest published scientific paper recorded in the Medline database as containing the specific term "signal transduction" within its text was published in 1972 Prior to 1977 articles can be found that use the term "signal transmission" or "sensory transduction" within their title or abstract. However, it was not until 1977 that papers began to be published with the specific term "signal transduction" within their abstract; it was not until 1979 that this term appeared within a paper title One source attributes the widespread use of the term signal transduction to a 1980 review article by Rodbell.

The occurrence of a specific term within the title or abstract of a scientific paper is usually a good indicator that the paper addresses a specifically related area of research.

While there may be considered to be a number of landmark or important discoveries in the field of signal transduction, such as the link made by Rodbell between metabolic regulation and the activity of GTP and GTP-binding proteins, much of our current understanding of signal transduction processes is as a result of numerous contributions made to the field over many years by different research groups all over the world.

The total number of scientific papers related to signal transduction published since 1st Jan 1977 up to the 31st December 2007 was 48,377 of which only 11,211 were reviews of other papers.

Signaling Molecules

Most signal transduction involves the binding of extracellular signaling molecules (or ligands) to cell-surface receptors that face outward from the plasma membrane and trigger events inside the cell. Also, intracellular signaling cascades can be triggered through cell-substratum interactions, as in the case of integrins, which bind ligands found within the extracellular matrix. Steroids represent another example of extracellular signaling molecules that may cross the plasma membrane due to their lipophilic or hydrophobic nature Many, but not all, steroids have receptors within the cytoplasm, and usually act by stimulating the binding of their receptors to the promoter region of steroid-responsive genes. Within multicellular organisms, there is a diverse number of small molecules and polypeptides that serve to coordinate a cell's individual biological activity within the context of the organism as a whole. These molecules have been functionally classified as:

- hormones (e.g., melatonin);
- growth factors (e.g. epidermal growth factor);
- extra-cellular matrix components (e.g., fibronectin);
- cytokines (e.g., interferon-gamma);
- chemokines (e.g., RANTES);
- neurotransmitters (e.g., acetylcholine); and
- neurotrophins (e.g., nerve growth factor).

It is important to note that most of these classifications do not take into account the molecular nature of each class member. For example, as a class, neurotransmitters consist of neuropeptides such as endorphins and small molecules such as serotonin and dopamine. Hormones are also a generic class of molecule able to initiate signal transduction, these include insulin (a polypeptide) testosterone (a steroid), and epinephrine (an amino acid derivative, in essence a small organic molecule).

The classification of one molecule into one class of another is not exact. For example, epinephrine and norepinephrine secreted by the central nervous system act as neurotransmitters. However, epinephrine when secreted by the adrenal medulla acts as a hormone.

Environmental Stimuli

In bacteria and other single-cell organisms, the variety of a signal transduction processes of which the cell is capable influences how many ways it can react and respond to its environment. In multicellular organisms, a multitude of different signal transduction processes are required for coordinating the behavior of individual cells to support the function of the organism as a whole. As may be expected, the more complex the organism, the more complex the repertoire of signal transduction processes the organism must possess. Thus, sensing of both the external and internal environments at the cellular level relies on signal transduction. Many disease processes such as diabetes, heart disease, autoimmunity, and cancer arise from defects in signal transduction pathways, further highlighting the critical importance of signal transduction to biology, as well as medicine.

In addition to many of the regular signal transduction stimuli listed above, in complex organisms, there are also examples of additional environmental stimuli that initiate signal transduction processes. Environmental stimuli may also be molecular in nature or more physical, such as light striking cells in the retina of the eye odorants binding to odorant receptors in the nasal epithelium and bitter and sweet tastes stimulating taste receptors in the taste buds Certain microbial molecules, e.g., viral nucleotides, bacterial lipopolysaccharides, and protein antigens, are able to elicit an immune system response against invading pathogens, mediated via signal transduction processes. An immune response may occur independent of signal transduction stimulation by other molecules, as is the case for signal transduction via the Toll-like receptor or with help from stimulatory molecules located at the cell surface of other cells, as is the case for T-cell receptor signalling.

Unicellular organisms may also respond to environmental stimuli via the activation of signal transduction pathways. For example, slime molds secrete cyclic-AMP upon starvation, which stimulates individual cells in the immediate environment to aggregate Yeast also use mating factors to determine the mating types of other yeast and participate in sexual reproduction.

Cellular Responses

Activation of genes alterations in metabolism the continued proliferation and death of the cell and the stimulation or suppression of locomotion are some of the cellular responses to extracellular stimulation that require signal transduction. Gene activation leads to further cellular effects, since the protein products of many of the responding genes include enzymes and transcription factors themselves. Transcription factors produced as a result of a signal transduction cascade can, in turn, activate yet more genes. Therefore, an initial stimulus can trigger the expression of an entire cohort of genes, and this, in turn, can lead to the activation of any number of complex physiological events. These events include the increased uptake of glucose from the blood stream stimulated by insulin and the migration of neutrophils to sites of infection stimulated by bacterial products. The set of genes and the order in which they are activated in response to stimuli are often referred to as a genetic programme.

Neurotransmitters are ligands that are capable of binding to ion channel proteins, resulting in their opening to allow the rapid flow of a particular ion across the plasma membrane This results in an altering of the cell's membrane potential and is important for processes such as the neural conduction of electrochemical impulses. Ligands can be freely soluble, or can be found on the surface of other cells or within the extracellular matrix. Such cell surface or extracellular matrix ligands signal between cells when they come in contact with each other, such as when a phagocytic cell presents antigens to lymphocytes, or upon adhesion to the extracellular matrix, as when integrins at the cell surface of fibroblasts engage fibronectin.

Most mammalian cells require stimulation to control not only cell division but also survival. In the absence of growth factor stimulation, programmed cell death ensues in most cells. Such requirements for extra-cellular stimulation are necessary for controlling cell behaviour in the context of both unicellular and multi-cellular organisms. Signal transduction pathways are perceived to be so central to biological processes that it is not surprising that a large number of diseases have been attributed to their disregulation.

Discussed below are how signal transduction via various classes of receptor may lead to the above cellular responses.

Types of Receptor

Receptors can be roughly divided into two major classes:

- Intracellular receptors; and
- Cell-surface receptors.

Ligand-gated ion channel receptors are a class of receptor that may occur both at the cell-surface or intracellularly.

Receptors that are solely intracellular include those for steroid hormones, thyroid hormone, retinoic acid, and derivatives of vitamin D3. In contrast to ligands that bind to cell surface receptors, in order to initiate signal transduction these ligands must cross the cell membrane.

Cell-surface Receptors

Cell-surface receptors are integral transmembrane proteins and recognize the vast majority of extracellular signaling molecules. Transmembrane receptors span the plasma membrane of the cell, with one part of the receptor on the outside of the cell (the extracellular domain), and the other on the inside of the cell (the intracellular domain). Signal transduction occurs as a result of stimulatory molecule or the binding of a ligand to its extracellular domain; the ligand itself does not pass through the plasma membrane prior to receptor-binding.

Binding of a ligand to a cell-surface receptor stimulates a series of events inside the cell, with different types of receptor stimulation of different intracellular responses. Receptors typically respond to only the binding of a specific ligand. Upon binding, the ligand initiates the transmission of a signal across the plasma membrane by inducing a change in the shape or conformation of the intracellular part of the receptor. Often, such changes in conformation either result in the activation of an enzymatic activity contained within the receptor or expose a binding site for other signaling proteins within the cell. Once these proteins bind to the receptor, they themselves may become active and propagate the signal into the cytoplasm.

In eukaryotic cells, most intracellular proteins activated by a ligand/receptor interaction possess an enzymatic activity. These enzymes include tyrosine kinase, heterotrimeric G proteins, small GTPases, various serine/threoine protein kinases, phosphatases, lipid kinases, and hydrolases. Some receptor-stimulated enzymes create specific second messengers including cyclic nucleotides, such as cyclic AMP (cAMP) and cyclic GMP (cGMP), Phosphatidylinositol derivatives, such as Phosphatidylinositol-triphosphate (PIP3), Diacylglycerol (DAG) and Inositol-triphosphate (IP3), IP3, controlling the release of intracellular calcium stores into the cytoplasm (see second messengers section later in this article). Other activated proteins interact with adapter proteins. Adapter proteins facilitate interactions between other signaling proteins, and coordinate the formation of signaling complexes necessary to produce an appropriate cellular response to a particular stimulus. Enzymes and adapter proteins are both responsive to various second messenger molecules.

Many of the enzymes activated as part of the signal transduction mechanism and also many adapter proteins have been found to possess specialized protein domains that bind to specific secondary messenger molecules. For example, calcium ions bind specifically to the EF hand domains of calmodulin, allowing this molecule to bind and activate Calmodulin-dependent kinase. PIP3, PIP2 and other phosphoinositides may bind to the Pleckstrin homology domains of proteins such as the kinase protein AKT again with activation activity.

There are many different classes of transmembrane receptor that recognize different extracellular signaling molecules. Specific example receptors discussed in this article are:

- G-protein coupled receptors, e.g., Chemokine receptors.
- Receptor tyrosine kinases, e.g., Growth factor receptors.
- Integrins.
- Toll-like receptors.

G-protein-coupled Receptors

Signal transduction from a G-protein-linked receptor following interaction with its hormone ligand G-protein-coupled receptors (GPCRs) are a family of integral membrane proteins that possess seven membrane-spanning domains, and are linked to a guanine nucleotide-binding protein (or heterotrimeric G protein). Many receptors make up this family, including adrenergic receptors, neurotransmitter receptors, olfactory receptors, opioid receptors, chemokine receptors, and rhodopsin.

Signal transduction by a GPCR begins with an inactive G protein coupled to the receptor. An inactive G protein exists as a heterotrimer, a molecule composed of three different protein subunits: Gα, Gß, and Gγ. Once the GPCR recognizes a ligand, the shape (conformation) of the receptor changes to mechanically activate the G protein, and causes one subunit (Gα) to bind a molecule of GTP (causing activation) and dissociate from the other two G-protein subunits (Gß and Gγ); the dissociation exposes sites on the G-protein subunits that interact with other molecules The activated G protein subunits detach from the receptor and initiate signaling from many downstream effector proteins, including phosphodiesterases and adenylyl cyclases, phospholipases, and ion channels that permit the release of second messenger molecules such as cyclic-AMP (cAMP), cyclic-GMP (cGMP), inositol triphosphate (IP3), diacylglycerol (DAG), and calcium (Ca^{2+}) ions For example, a rhodopsin molecule in the plasma membrane of a retina cell in the eye that was activated by a photon can activate up to 2000 effector molecules (in this case, transducin) per second.

The total strength of signal amplification by a GPCR is determined by:

- The lifetime of the ligand-receptor-complex. If the ligand-receptor-complex is stable, it takes longer for the ligand to dissociate from its receptor, thus the receptor will remain active for longer and will activate more effector proteins.
- The amount and lifetime of the receptor-effector protein-complex. The more effector protein is available to be activated by the receptor, and the faster the activated effector protein can dissociate from the receptor, the more effector protein will be activated in the same amount of time.

Deactivation of the activated receptor. A receptor that is engaged in a hormone-receptor-complex can be deactivated, either by covalent modification (for example, phosphorylation) or by internalization.

Deactivation of effectors through intrinsic enzymatic activity. Either small or large G-proteins possess intrinsic GTPase activity, which controls the duration of the triggered signal. This activity may be increased through the action of other proteins such as GTPase-activating proteins (GAPS).

The idea that G-protein-coupled receptors, to be specific, chemokine receptors, participate in cancer development is suggested by a study wherein a point mutation was inserted into the gene encoding the chemokine receptor CXCR2. Cells transfected with the CXCR2 mutant underwent a malignant transformation The result of the point mutation was the expression of CXCR2 in an active conformation, despite the absence of chemokine-binding (the CXCR2 mutant is said to be "constitutively active").

Receptor Tyrosine Kinases

Receptor tyrosine kinases (RTKs) are transmembrane proteins with an intracellular kinase domain and an extracellular domain that binds ligand. There are many RTK proteins that are classified into subfamilies depending on their structural properties and ligand specificity. These include many growth factor receptors such as insulin receptor and the insulin-like growth factor receptors, and many others receptors To conduct their biochemical signals, RTKs need to form dimers in the plasma membrane The dimer is stabilized by ligand binding by the receptor. Interaction between the two cytoplasmic domains of the dimer is thought to stimulate autophosphorylation of tyrosines within the cytoplasmic tyrosine kinase domains of the RTKs causing their conformational changes. The kinase domain of the receptors is subsequently activated, initiating signaling cascades of phosphorylation of downstream cytoplasmic molecules. These signals are essential to various cellular processes, such as control of cell growth, differentiation, metabolism, and migration.

As is the case with G-Protein-coupled receptors, proteins that bind GTP play a major role in transmission of signal from the activated RTK into the cell. In this case, the G proteins are members of the Ras, Rho, and Raf families, referred to collectively as small G proteins. These proteins act as molecular switches that are usually tethered to membranes by isoprenyl groups linked to their carboxyl ends. Thus, upon activation, they are responsible for the recruitment of proteins to specific membrane subdomains where they participate in signaling. Activated RTKs, in turn, activate small G proteins, which in turn activate Guanine Nucleotide Exchange Factors, such as SOS1. Once activated, these exchange factors can activate many more small G-proteins, thus amplifying the receptors initial signal.

As with the mutation of G-protein coupled receptors, the mutation of certain RTK genes can result in the expression of receptors that exist in a constitutively-activate state. Such mutated RTK genes may act as oncogenes, genes that contribute to the initiation or progression of cancer.

Integrins

Integrins are produced by a wide variety of cell types, and play a role in the attachment of a cell to the extracellular matrix (ECM) and to other cells, and in the signal transduction of signals received from extracellular matrix components such as fibronectin, collagen, and laminin. Ligand-binding to the extracellular domain of integrins induces a conformational change within the protein and a clustering of the protein at the cell surface, in order to initiate signal transduction. Integrins lack kinase activity, and integrin-mediated signal transduction is achieved through a variety of intracellular protein kinases and adaptor molecules such as integrin-linked kinase (ILK), focal-adhesion kinase (FAK), talin, paxillin, parvins, p130Cas, Src-family kinases, and GTPases of the Rho family, the main protein coordinating signal transduction being ILK. As shown in the overview to the right, cooperative integrin and receptor tyrosine kinase signaling determine cellular survival, apoptosis, proliferation, and differentiation.

Important differences exist between integrin-signaling in circulating blood cells and that in non-circulating blood cells such as epithelial cells. Integrins at the cell-surface of circulating cells are inactive under normal physiological conditions. For example, cell-surface integrins on circulating leukocytes are maintained in an inactive state in order to avoid epithelial cell attachment. Only in response to appropriate stimuli are leukocyte integrins converted into an active form, such as those received at the site of an inflammatory response. In a similar manner, it is important that integrins at the cell surface of circulating platelets are kept in an inactive state under normal conditions, in order to avoid thrombosis. Epithelial cells, in contrast, have active integrins at their cell surface under normal conditions, which help to maintain their stable adhesion to underlying stromal cells, which provide appropriate signals in order to maintain their survival and differentiation.

Toll-like Receptors

When activated, Toll-like receptors (TLRs) recruit adapter molecules within the cytoplasm of cells in order to propagate a signal. Four adapter molecules are known to be involved in signaling. These proteins are known as MyD88, Tirap (also called Mal), Trif, and Tram. The adapters activate other molecules within the cell, including certain protein kinases (IRAK1, IRAK4, TBK1, and IKKi) that amplify the signal, and ultimately lead to the induction or suppression of genes that orchestrate the inflammatory response. In all, thousands of genes are activated by TLR signaling, and, together, the TLRs constitute one of the most powerful and important gateways for gene modulation.

Ligand-gated Ion Channel Receptors

A ligand-activated ion channel will recognize its ligand, and then undergo a structural change that opens a gap (channel) in the plasma membrane through which ions can pass. These ions will then relay the signal. An example for this mechanism is found in the receiving cell, or post-synaptic cell of a neural synapse.

By contrast, other ion channels open in response to a change in cell potential, that is, the difference of the electrical charge across the membrane. In neurons, this mechanism underlies the action potentials that travel along nerves. The influx of ions that occurs in response to ligand-gated ion channels often induce action potentials by depolarizing the membrane of the post-synaptic cells, which results in the wave-like opening of voltage-gated ion channels. In addition, calcium ions are also commonly allowed into the cell during ligand-induced ion channel opening. This calcium can act as a classical second messenger, setting in motion signal transduction cascades and altering the cellular physiology of the responding cell. This may result in strengthening of the synapse between the pre- and post-synaptic cells by remodeling the dendritic spines involved in the synapse.

Intracellular Receptors

Intracellular receptors include nuclear receptors and cytoplasmic receptors, and are soluble proteins localized within the nucleoplasm or the cytoplasm, respectively. The typical ligands for nuclear receptors are lipophilic hormones, with steroid hormones (for example, testosterone, progesterone, and cortisol) and derivatives of vitamin A and D among them. In order to reach its receptor and initiate signal transduction, the hormone must pass through the plasma membrane, usually by passive diffusion. The nuclear receptors are ligand-activated transcription activators; on binding with the ligand (the hormone), the ligands will pass through the nuclear membrane into the nucleus and enable the transcription of a certain gene and, thus, the production of a protein.

The nuclear receptors that were activated by the hormones attach at the DNA at receptor-specific Hormone-

Responsive Elements (HREs), DNA sequences that are located in the promoter region of the genes that are activated by the hormone-receptor complex. As this enables the transcription of the according gene, these hormones are also called inductors of gene expression. The activation of gene transcription is much slower than signals that directly affect existing proteins. As a consequence, the effects of hormones that use nucleic receptors are usually long-term. Although the signal transduction via these soluble receptors involves only a few proteins, the details of gene regulation are yet not well understood. The nucleic receptors all have a similar, modular structure:

N-AAAABBBBCCCCDDDDEEEEFFFF-C

Where CCCC is the DNA-binding domain that contains zinc fingers, and EEEE the ligand-binding domain. The latter is also responsible for dimerization of most nuclearic receptors prior to DNA binding. As a third function, it contains structural elements that are responsible for transactivation, used for communication with the translational apparatus. The zinc fingers in the DNA-binding domain stabilize DNA binding by holding contact to the phosphate backbone of the DNA. The DNA sequences that match the receptor are usually hexameric repeats, either normal, inverted, or everted. The sequences are quite similar, but their orientation and distance are the parameters by which the DNA-binding domains of the receptors can tell them apart.

Steroid receptors are a subclass of nuclear receptors, located primarily within the cytosol. In the absence of steroid hormone, the receptors cling together in a complex called an aporeceptor complex, which also contains chaperone proteins (also known as *heatshock proteins* or *Hsps*). The Hsps are necessary to activate the receptor by assisting the protein to fold in a way such that the signal sequence that enables its passage into the nucleus is accessible.

Steroid receptors can also have a repressive effect on gene expression, when their transactivation domain is hidden so it cannot activate transcription. Furthermore, steroid receptor activity can be enhanced by phosphorylation of serine residues at their N-terminal end, as a result of another signal transduction pathway, for example, a by a growth factor. This behaviour is called crosstalk.

RXR- and orphan-receptors: These nuclear receptors can be activated by:

- a classic endocrine-synthesized hormone that entered the cell by diffusion;
- a hormone that was built within the cell (for example, retinol) from a precursor or prohormone, which can be brought to the cell through the bloodstream; and
- a hormone that was completely synthesized within the cell, for example, prostaglandin.

These receptors are located in the nucleus and are not accompanied by chaperone proteins. In the absence of hormone, they bind to their specific DNA sequence, repressing the gene. Upon activation by the hormone, they activate the transcription of the gene that they were repressing.

Certain intracellular receptors of the immune system are examples of cytoplasmic receptors. Recently-identified NOD like receptors (NLRs) reside in the cytoplasm of specific eukaryotic cells and interact with particular ligands, such as microbial molecules, using a leucine-rich repeat (LRR) motif that is similar to the ligand-binding motif of the extracellular receptors known as TLRs. Some of these molecules (e.g., NOD1 and NOD2) interact with an enzyme called RICK kinase (or RIP2 kinase) that activates NF-?B signaling, whereas others (e.g., NALP3) interact with inflammatory caspases (e.g., caspase 1) and initiate processing of particular cytokines (e.g., interleukin-1ß) Similar receptors exist inside plant cells and are called Plant R Proteins. Another type of cytoplasmic receptor also has a role in immune surveillance. These receptors are known as RNA Helicases and include RIG-I, MDA5, and LGP2.

SECOND MESSENGERS

Intracellular signal transduction is largely carried out by second messenger molecules.

Calcium

Ca^{2+} concentration is usually maintained at a very low level in the cytosol by sequestration in the smooth endoplasmic reticulum and the mitochondria. Ca^{2+} release from the endoplasmic reticulum into the cytosol results in the binding of the released Ca^{2+} to signaling proteins that are then activated. There are two combined receptor/ion channel proteins that perform the task of controlled transport of Ca^{2+}.

- The InsP3-receptor will transport Ca^{2+} upon interaction with inositol triphosphate (thus the name) on its cytosolic side. It consists of four identical subunits.
- The ryanodine receptor is named after the plant alkaloid ryanodine. It is similar to the InsP3 receptor and stimulated to transport Ca^{2+} into the cytosol by recognizing Ca^{2+} on its cytosolic side, thus establishing a feedback mechanism; a small amount of Ca^{2+} in the cytosol near the receptor will cause it to release even more Ca^{2+}. It is especially important in neurons and muscle cells. In heart and pancreas cells, another second messenger (cyclic-ADP ribose) takes part in the receptor activation. The localized and time-limited activity of Ca^{2+} in the cytosol is also called a Ca^{2+} wave. Once released into the cytosol from intracellular stores or extracellular sources, Ca^{2+} acts as a signal molecule within the cell. This works by tightly limiting the time and space when Ca^{2+} is free (and thus active). Therefore,

the concentration of free Ca^{2+} within the cell is usually very low; it is stored within organelles, usually the endoplasmic reticulum (sarcoplasmic reticulum in muscle cells), where it is bound to molecules like calreticulin.

Ca^{2+} is used in a multitude of processes, among them muscle contraction, release of neurotransmitter from nerve endings, vision in retina cells, proliferation, secretion, cytoskeleton management, cell migration, gene expression, and metabolism. The three main pathways that lead to Ca^{2+} activation are :

1. G protein-regulated pathways.
2. Pathways regulated by receptor-tyrosine kinases.
3. Ligand- or current-regulated ion channels.

There are two different ways by which Ca^{2+} can regulate proteins:

1. A direct recognition of Ca^{2+} by the protein.
2. Binding of Ca^{2+} in the active site of an enzyme.

One of the best-studied interactions of Ca^{2+} with a protein is the regulation of calmodulin by Ca^{2+}. Calmodulin itself can regulate other proteins, or be part of a larger protein (for example, phosphorylase kinase). The Ca^{2+}/calmodulin complex plays an important role in proliferation, mitosis, and neural signal transduction.

Lipophilic

Lipophilic second messenger molecules - These molecules are all derived from lipids that normally reside in cellular membranes. Enzymes stimulated by activated receptors modify these lipids, converting them into second messengers. One example of lipophilic second messenger molecule is diacylglycerol, required for the activation of protein kinase C. Others are ceramide, the eicosanoids, and lysophosphatidic acid.

Nitric Oxide

The gas nitric oxide (NO) is a free radical that diffuses through the plasma membrane and affects nearby cells. NO is made from arginine and oxygen by the enzyme NO synthase, with citrulline as a by-product. NO works mainly through activation of its target receptor, the enzyme soluble guanylate cyclase, which, when activated, produces the second messenger cyclic-guanosine mono-phosphate (cGMP). NO can also act through covalent modification of proteins or their metal cofactors. Some of these modifications are reversible and work through a redox mechanism. In high concentrations, NO is toxic, and is thought to be responsible for some damage after a stroke. NO serves multiple functions. These include:

- Relaxation of blood vessels.
- Regulation of exocytosis of neurotransmitters.
- Cellular immune response.
- Modulation of the Hair Cycle.
- Production and maintenance of penile erections.
- Activation of apoptosis by initiating signals that lead to H2AX phosphorylation.

CHAPTER

7

Protein

Proteins are organic compounds made of amino acids arranged in a linear chain and joined together by peptide bonds between the carboxyl and amino groups of adjacent amino acid residues. The sequence of amino acids in a protein is defined by the sequence of a gene, which is encoded in the genetic code In general, the genetic code specifies 20 standard amino acids, however in certain organisms the genetic code can include selenocysteine - and in certain archaea - pyrrolysine. The residues in a protein are often observed to be chemically modified by post-translational modification, which can happen either before the protein is used in the cell, or as part of control mechanisms. Proteins can also work together to achieve a particular function, and they often associate to form stable complexes.

Like other biological macromolecules such as polysaccharides and nucleic acids, proteins are essential parts of organisms and participate in every process within cells. Many proteins are enzymes that catalyze biochemical reactions and are vital to metabolism. Proteins also have structural or mechanical functions, such as actin and myosin in muscle and the proteins in the cytoskeleton, which form a system of scaffolding that maintains cell shape. Other proteins are important in cell signaling, immune responses, cell adhesion, and the cell cycle. Proteins are also necessary in animals' diets, since animals cannot synthesize all the amino acids they need and must obtain essential amino acids from food. Through the process of digestion, animals break down ingested protein into free amino acids that are then used in metabolism.

The word 'protein' comes from the Greek word (*proteios*) "primary". Proteins were first described and named by the Swedish chemist Jöns Jakob Berzelius in 1838. However, the central role of proteins in living organisms was not fully appreciated until 1926, when James B. Sumner showed that the enzyme urease was a protein. The first protein to be sequenced was insulin, by Frederick Sanger, who won the Nobel Prize for this achievement in 1958. The first protein structures to be solved included hemoglobin and myoglobin, by Max Perutz and Sir John Cowdery Kendrew, respectively, in 1958 The three-dimensional structures of both proteins were first determined by x-ray diffraction analysis; Perutz and Kendrew shared the 1962 Nobel Prize in Chemistry for these discoveries.

The amino acids in a polypeptide chain are linked by peptide bonds. Once linked in the protein chain, an individual amino acid is called a residue, and the linked series of carbon, nitrogen, and oxygen atoms are known as the main chain or protein backbone. The peptide bond has two resonance forms that contribute some double-bond character and inhibit rotation around its axis, so that the alpha carbons are roughly coplanar. The other two dihedral angles in the peptide bond determine the local shape assumed by the protein backbone.

SYNTHESIS

Proteins are assembled from amino acids using information encoded in genes. Each protein has its own unique amino acid sequence that is specified by the nucleotide sequence of the gene encoding this protein. The genetic code is a set of three-nucleotide sets called codons and each three-nucleotide combination stands for an amino acid, for example AUG stands for methionine. Because DNA contains four nucleotides, the total number of possible codons is 64; hence, there is some redundancy in the genetic code, with some amino acids specified by more than one codon. Genes encoded in DNA are first transcribed into pre-messenger RNA (mRNA) by proteins such as RNA polymerase. Most organisms then process the pre-mRNA (also known as a primary transcript) using various forms of post-transcriptional modification to form the mature mRNA, which is then used as a template for protein synthesis by the ribosome. In prokaryotes the mRNA may either be used as soon as it is produced, or be bound by a ribosome after having moved away from the nucleoid. In contrast, eukaryotes make mRNA in the cell nucleus and then translocate it across the nuclear membrane into the cytoplasm, where protein synthesis then takes place. The rate of protein synthesis is higher in prokaryotes than eukaryotes and can reach up to 20 amino acids per second.

The process of synthesizing a protein from an mRNA template is known as translation. The mRNA is loaded onto the ribosome and is read three nucleotides at a time by matching each codon to its base pairing anticodon located on a transfer RNA molecule, which carries the amino acid corresponding to the codon it recognizes. The enzyme aminoacyl tRNA synthetase "charges" the tRNA molecules with the correct amino acids. The growing polypeptide is often termed the nascent chain. Proteins are always biosynthesized from N-terminus to C-terminus.

The size of a synthesized protein can be measured by the number of amino acids it contains and by its total molecular mass, which is normally reported in units of daltons (synonymous with atomic mass units), or the derivative unit kilodalton (kDa). Yeast proteins are on average 466 amino acids long and 53 kDa in mass The largest known proteins are the titins, a component of the muscle sarcomere, with a molecular mass of almost 3,000 kDa and a total length of almost 27,000 amino acids.

Chemical Synthesis

Three possible representations of the three-dimensional structure of the protein triose phosphate isomerase. Left: all-atom representation colored by atom type. Middle: simplified representation illustrating the backbone conformation, colored by secondary structure. Right: Solvent-accessible surface representation colored by residue type (acidic residues red, basic residues blue, polar residues green, nonpolar residues white).Most proteins fold into unique 3-dimensional structures. The shape into which a protein naturally folds is known as its native state. Although many proteins can fold unassisted, simply through the chemical properties of their amino acids, others require the aid of molecular chaperones to fold into their native states. Biochemists often refer to four distinct aspects of a protein's structure:

- *Primary structure:* the amino acid sequence.
- *Secondary structure:* regularly repeating local structures stabilized by hydrogen bonds. The most common examples are the alpha helix and beta sheet Because secondary structures are local, many regions of different secondary structure can be present in the same protein molecule.
- *Tertiary structure:* the overall shape of a single protein molecule; the spatial relationship of the secondary

structures to one another. Tertiary structure is generally stabilized by nonlocal interactions, most commonly the formation of a hydrophobic core, but also through salt bridges, hydrogen bonds, disulfide bonds, and even post-translational modifications. The term "tertiary structure" is often used as synonymous with the term fold. The Tertiary structure is what controls the basic function of the protein.

- *Quaternary structure:* the shape or structure that results from the interaction of more than one protein molecule, usually called protein subunits in this context, which function as part of the larger assembly or protein complex.

Proteins are not entirely rigid molecules. In addition to these levels of structure, proteins may shift between several related structures while they perform their functions. In the context of these functional rearrangements, these tertiary or quaternary structures are usually referred to as "conformations", and transitions between them are called conformational changes. Such changes are often induced by the binding of a substrate molecule to an enzyme's active site, or the physical region of the protein that participates in chemical catalysis. In solution all proteins also undergo variation in structure through thermal vibration and the collision with other molecules.

Proteins can be informally divided into three main classes, which correlate with typical tertiary structures: globular proteins, fibrous proteins, and membrane proteins. Almost all globular proteins are soluble and many are enzymes. Fibrous proteins are often structural; membrane proteins often serve as receptors or provide channels for polar or charged molecules to pass through the cell membrane.

A special case of intramolecular hydrogen bonds within proteins, poorly shielded from water attack and hence promoting their own dehydration, are called dehydrons.

Structure Determination

Discovering the tertiary structure of a protein, or the quaternary structure of its complexes, can provide important clues about how the protein performs its function. Common experimental methods of structure determination include X-ray crystallography and NMR spectroscopy, both of which can produce information at atomic resolution. Cryoelectron microscopy is used to produce lower-resolution structural information about very large protein complexes, including assembled viruses; a variant known as electron crystallography can also produce high-resolution information in some cases, especially for two-dimensional crystals of membrane proteins. Solved structures are usually deposited in the Protein Data Bank (PDB), a freely available resource from which structural data about thousands of proteins can be obtained in the form of Cartesian coordinates for each atom in the protein.

Many more gene sequences are known than protein structures. Further, the set of solved structures is biased toward proteins that can be easily subjected to the conditions required in X-ray crystallography, one of the major structure determination methods. In particular, globular proteins are comparatively easy to crystallize in preparation for X-ray crystallography. Membrane proteins, by contrast, are difficult to crystallize and are underrepresented in the PDB. Structural genomics initiatives have attempted to remedy these deficiencies by systematically solving representative structures of major fold classes. Protein structure prediction methods attempt to provide a means of generating a plausible structure for proteins whose structures have not been experimentally determined.

CELLULAR FUNCTIONS

Proteins are the chief actors within the cell, said to be carrying out the duties specified by the information encoded in genes With the exception of certain types of RNA, most other biological molecules are relatively inert elements upon which proteins act. Proteins make up half the dry weight of an Escherichia coli cell, whereas other macromolecules such as DNA and RNA make up only 3% and 20%, respectively. The set of proteins expressed in a particular cell or cell type is known as its proteome.

The chief characteristic of proteins that allows their diverse set of functions is their ability to bind other molecules specifically and tightly. The region of the protein responsible for binding another molecule is known as the binding site and is often a depression or "pocket" on the molecular surface. This binding ability is mediated by the tertiary structure of the protein, which defines the binding site pocket, and by the chemical properties of the surrounding amino acids' side chains. Protein binding can be extraordinarily tight and specific; for example, the ribonuclease inhibitor protein binds to human angiogenin with a sub-femtomolar dissociation constant (<10-15 M) but does not bind at all to its amphibian homolog onconase (>1 M). Extremely minor chemical changes such as the addition of a single methyl group to a binding partner can sometimes suffice to nearly eliminate binding; for example, the aminoacyl tRNA synthetase specific to the amino acid valine discriminates against the very similar side chain of the amino acid isoleucine.

Proteins can bind to other proteins as well as to small-molecule substrates. When proteins bind specifically to other copies of the same molecule, they can oligomerize to form fibrils; this process occurs often in structural proteins that consist of globular monomers that self-associate to form rigid fibers. Protein-protein interactions also regulate enzymatic activity, control progression through the cell cycle, and allow the assembly of large protein complexes that carry out many closely related reactions with a common biological function. Proteins can also bind to, or even be integrated into, cell membranes. The ability of binding partners to induce conformational changes in proteins allows the construction of enormously complex signaling networks.

Enzymes

The best-known role of proteins in the cell is as enzymes, which catalyze chemical reactions. Enzymes are usually highly specific and accelerate only one or a few chemical reactions. Enzymes carry out most of the reactions involved in metabolism, as well as manipulating DNA in processes such as DNA replication, DNA repair, and transcription. Some enzymes act on other proteins to add or remove chemical groups in a process known as post-translational modification. About 4,000 reactions are known to be catalyzed by enzymes. The rate acceleration conferred by enzymatic catalysis is often enormous - as much as 1017-fold increase in rate over the uncatalyzed reaction in the case of orotate decarboxylase (78 million years without the enzyme, 18 milliseconds with the enzyme).

The molecules bound and acted upon by enzymes are called substrates. Although enzymes can consist of hundreds of amino acids, it is usually only a small fraction of the residues that come in contact with the substrate, and an even smaller fraction - 3-4 residues on average - that are directly involved in catalysis. The region of the enzyme that binds the substrate and contains the catalytic residues is known as the active site.

Cell Signalling and Ligand Binding

A mouse antibody against cholera that binds a carbohydrate antigen.Many proteins are involved in the process of cell signaling and signal transduction. Some proteins, such as insulin, are extracellular proteins that transmit a signal from the cell in which they were synthesized to other cells in distant tissues. Others are membrane proteins that act as receptors whose main function is to bind a signaling molecule and induce a biochemical response in the cell. Many receptors have a binding site exposed on the cell surface and an effector domain within the cell, which may have enzymatic activity or may undergo a conformational change detected by other proteins within the cell.

Antibodies are protein components of adaptive immune system whose main function is to bind antigens, or foreign substances in the body, and target them for destruction. Antibodies can be secreted into the extracellular environment or anchored in the membranes of specialized B cells known as plasma cells. Whereas enzymes are limited in their binding affinity for their substrates by the necessity of conducting their reaction, antibodies have no such constraints. An antibody's binding affinity to its target is extraordinarily high.

Many ligand transport proteins bind particular small biomolecules and transport them to other locations in the body of a multicellular organism. These proteins must have a high binding affinity when their ligand is present in high concentrations, but must also release the ligand when it is present at low concentrations in the target tissues. The canonical example of a ligand-binding protein is haemoglobin, which transports oxygen from the lungs to other organs and tissues in all vertebrates and has close homologs in every biological kingdom. Lectins are sugar-binding proteins which are highly specific for their sugar moieties. Lectins typically play a role in biological recognition phenomena involving cells and proteins. Receptors and hormones are highly specific binding proteins.

Transmembrane proteins can also serve as ligand transport proteins that alter the permeability of the cell membrane to small molecules and ions. The membrane alone has a hydrophobic core through which polar or charged molecules cannot diffuse. Membrane proteins contain internal channels that allow such molecules to enter and exit the cell.

Many ion channel proteins are specialized to select for only a particular ion; for example, potassium and sodium channels often discriminate for only one of the two ions.

Structural Proteins

Structural proteins confer stiffness and rigidity to otherwise-fluid biological components. Most structural proteins are fibrous proteins; for example, actin and tubulin are globular and soluble as monomers, but polymerize to form long, stiff fibers that comprise the cytoskeleton, which allows the cell to maintain its shape and size. Collagen and elastin are critical components of connective tissue such as cartilage, and keratin is found in hard or filamentous structures such as hair, nails, feathers, hooves, and some animal shells.

Other proteins that serve structural functions are motor proteins such as myosin, kinesin, and dynein, which are capable of generating mechanical forces. These proteins are crucial for cellular motility of single celled organisms and the sperm of many sexually reproducing multicellular organisms. They also generate the forces exerted by contracting muscles.

As some of the most commonly studied biological molecules, the activities and structures of proteins are examined both in vitro and in vivo. In vitro studies of purified proteins in controlled environments are useful for learning how a protein carries out its function: for example, enzyme kinetics studies explore the chemical mechanism of an enzyme's catalytic activity and its relative affinity for various possible substrate molecules. By contrast, in vivo experiments on proteins' activities within cells or even within whole organisms can provide complementary information about where a protein functions and how it is regulated.

Protein Purification

In order to perform in vitro analysis, a protein must be purified away from other cellular components. This process usually begins with cell lysis, in which a cell's membrane is disrupted and its internal contents released into a solution known as a crude lysate. The resulting mixture can be purified using ultracentrifugation, which fractionates the various cellular components into fractions containing soluble proteins; membrane lipids and proteins; cellular organelles, and nucleic acids. Precipitation by a method known as salting out can concentrate the proteins from this lysate. Various types of chromatography are then used to isolate the protein or proteins of interest based on properties such as molecular weight, net charge and binding affinity. The level of purification can be monitored using various types of gel electrophoresis if the desired protein's molecular weight and isoelectric point are known, by spectroscopy if the protein has distinguishable spectroscopic features, or by enzyme assays if the protein has enzymatic activity. Additionally, proteins can be isolated according their charge using electrofocusing.

For natural proteins, a series of purification steps may be necessary to obtain protein sufficiently pure for laboratory applications. To simplify this process, genetic engineering is often used to add chemical features to proteins that make them easier to purify without affecting their structure or activity. Here, a "tag" consisting of a specific amino acid sequence, often a series of histidine residues (a "His-tag"), is attached to one terminus of the protein. As a result, when the lysate is passed over a chromatography column containing nickel, the histidine residues ligate the nickel and attach to the column while the untagged components of the lysate pass unimpeded.

CELLULAR LOCALIZATION

The study of proteins in vivo is often concerned with the synthesis and localization of the protein within the cell. Although many intracellular proteins are synthesized in the cytoplasm and membrane-bound or secreted proteins in the endoplasmic reticulum, the specifics of how proteins are targeted to specific organelles or cellular structures is often unclear. A useful technique for assessing cellular localization uses genetic engineering to express in a cell a fusion protein or chimera consisting of the natural protein of interest linked to a "reporter" such as green fluorescent protein (GFP). The fused protein's position within the cell can be cleanly and efficiently visualized using microscopy, as shown in the figure opposite. In these cases, additional fluorescent chimeric proteins are generally required to prove the inferred localization.

Other methods for elucidating the cellular location of proteins requires the use of known compartmental markers for regions such as the ER, the Golgi, lysosomes/vacuoles, mitochondria, chloroplasts, plasma membrane, etc. With the use of fluorescently-tagged versions of these markers or of antibodies to known markers, it becomes much simpler to identify the localization of a protein of interest. For example, indirect immunofluorescence will allow for fluorescence colocalization and demonstration of location. Fluorescent dyes are used to label cellular compartments for a similar purpose.

Other possibilities exist, as well. For example, immunohistochemistry usually utilizes an antibody to one or more proteins of interest that are conjugated to enzymes yielding either luminescent or chromogenic signals that can be compared between samples, allowing for localization information. Another applicable technique is cofractionation in sucrose (or other material) gradients using isopycnic centrifugation. While this technique does not prove colocalization of a compartment of known density and the protein of interest, it does increase the likelihood, and is more amenable to large-scale studies.

Finally, the gold-standard method of cellular localization is immunoelectron microscopy. This technique also uses an antibody to the protein of interest, along with classical electron microscopy techniques. The sample is prepared for normal electron microscopic examination, and then treated with an antibody to the protein of interest that is conjugated to an extremely electro-dense material, usually gold. This allows for the localization of both ultrastructural details as well as the protein of interest.

Through another genetic engineering application known as site-directed mutagenesis, researchers can alter the protein sequence and hence its structure, cellular localization, and susceptibility to regulation, which can be followed in vivo by GFP tagging or in vitro by enzyme kinetics and binding studies.

PROTEOMICS AND BIOINFORMATICS

The total complement of proteins present at a time in a cell or cell type is known as its proteome, and the study of such large-scale data sets defines the field of proteomics, named by analogy to the related field of genomics. Key experimental techniques in proteomics include 2D electrophoresis, which allows the separation of a large number of proteins, mass spectrometry, which allows rapid high-throughput identification of proteins and sequencing of peptides (most often after in-gel digestion), protein microarrays, which allow the detection of the relative levels of a large number of proteins present in a cell, and two-hybrid screening, which allows the systematic exploration of protein-protein interactions. The total complement of biologically possible such interactions is known as the interactome. A systematic attempt to determine the structures of proteins representing every possible fold is known as structural genomics.

The large amount of genomic and proteomic data available for a variety of organisms, including the human genome, allows researchers to efficiently identify homologous proteins in distantly related organisms by sequence alignment. Sequence profiling tools can perform more specific sequence manipulations such as restriction enzyme maps, open reading frame analyses for nucleotide sequences, and secondary structure prediction. From this data phylogenetic trees can be constructed and evolutionary hypotheses developed using special software like ClustalW regarding the ancestry of modern organisms and the genes they express. The field of bioinformatics seeks to assemble, annotate, and analyze genomic and proteomic data, applying computational techniques to biological problems such as gene finding and cladistics.

STRUCTURE PREDICTION AND SIMULATION

Complementary to the field of structural genomics, protein structure prediction seeks to develop efficient ways to provide plausible models for proteins whose structures have not yet been determined experimentally The most successful type of structure prediction, known as homology modeling, relies on the existence of a "template" structure with sequence similarity to the protein being modeled; structural genomics' goal is to provide sufficient representation in solved structures to model most of those that remain. Although producing accurate models remains a challenge when only distantly related template structures are available, it has been suggested that sequence alignment is the bottleneck in this process, as quite accurate models can be produced if a "perfect" sequence alignment is known Many structure prediction methods have served to inform the emerging field of protein engineering, in which novel protein folds have already been designed. A more complex computational problem is the prediction of intermolecular interactions, such as in molecular docking and protein-protein interaction prediction.

The processes of protein folding and binding can be simulated using techniques derived from molecular dynamics. The folding of small alpha-helical protein domains such as the villin headpiece and the HIV accessory protein have been successfully simulated in silico, and hybrid methods that combine standard molecular dynamics with quantum mechanics calculations have allowed exploration of the electronic states of rhodopsins.

NUTRITION

Most microorganisms and plants can biosynthesize all 20 standard amino acids, while animals (including humans) must obtain some of the amino acids from the diet.

The amino acids that an organism cannot synthesize on its own are referred to as essential amino acids. Key enzymes that synthesize certain amino acids are not present in animals - such as aspartokinase, which catalyzes the first step in the synthesis of lysine, methionine, and threonine from aspartate. If amino acids are present in the environment, microorganisms can conserve energy by taking up the amino acids from their surroundings and downregulating their biosynthetic pathways.

In animals, amino acids are obtained through the consumption of foods containing protein. Ingested proteins are broken down through digestion, which typically involves denaturation of the protein through exposure to acid and hydrolysis by enzymes called proteases. Some ingested amino acids are used for protein biosynthesis, while others are converted to glucose through gluconeogenesis, or fed into the citric acid cycle. This use of protein as a fuel is particularly important under starvation conditions as it allows the body's own proteins to be used to support life, particularly those found in muscle Amino acids are also an important dietary source of nitrogen.

Proteins were recognized as a distinct class of biological molecules in the eighteenth century by Antoine Fourcroy and others, distinguished by the molecules' ability to coagulate or flocculate under treatments with heat or acid. Noted examples at the time included albumin from egg whites, blood, serum albumin, fibrin, and wheat gluten. Dutch chemist Gerhardus Johannes Mulder carried out elemental analysis of common proteins and found that nearly all proteins had the same empirical formula. The term "protein" to describe these molecules was proposed in 1838 by

Mulder's associate Jöns Jakob Berzelius. Mulder went on to identify the products of protein degradation such as the amino acid leucine for which he found a (nearly correct) molecular weight of 131 Da.

The difficulty in purifying proteins in large quantities made them very difficult for early protein biochemists to study. Hence, early studies focused on proteins that could be purified in large quantities, e.g., those of blood, egg white, various toxins, and digestive/metabolic enzymes obtained from slaughterhouses. In the late 1950s, the Armour Hot Dog Co. purified 1 kg (= one million milligrams) of pure bovine pancreatic ribonuclease A and made it freely available to scientists around the world.

Linus Pauling is credited with the successful prediction of regular protein secondary structures based on hydrogen bonding, an idea first put forth by William Astbury in 1933. Later work by Walter Kauzmann on denaturation, based partly on previous studies by Kaj Linderstrøm-Lang, contributed an understanding of protein folding and structure mediated by hydrophobic interactions. In 1949 Fred Sanger correctly determined the amino acid sequence of insulin, thus conclusively demonstrating that proteins consisted of linear polymers of amino acids rather than branched chains, colloids, or cyclols. The first atomic-resolution structures of proteins were solved by X-ray crystallography in the 1960s and by NMR in the 1980s. As of 2006, the Protein Data Bank has nearly 40,000 atomic-resolution structures of proteins. In more recent times, cryo-electron microscopy of large macromolecular assemblies and computational protein structure prediction of small protein domains are two methods approaching atomic resolution.

List of Proteins

- A list of proteins (and protein complexes). This list aims to organize information on the protein universe.

- All proteins can be found in the human proteome unless marked with a "%".

Cytoskeletal Proteins

actin	myosin
dystrophin	Tau (protein)
FtsZ %	tubulin
keratin	spectrin

Extracellular matrix proteins

Collagen	Reelin
Elastin	F-spondin

Globular Proteins

Plasma proteins

Serum albumin	Serum Amyloid P Component

Coagulation Factors

Factor XIII	von Willebrand Factor
Factor VIII	Protein C
	Protein Z
	Protein Z-related protease inhibitor
	Protein S

Complement proteins

C1-inhibitor

C3-convertase

Acute phase proteins

C-reactive protein

Hemoproteins

Cell adhesion

cadherin

integrin

NCAM

selectin

Transmembrane Transport Proteins

Ion pumping enzymes are in the enzymes section.

CFTR

Glycophorin D

Scramblase

Ion Channels

Acetylcholine receptor

Nicotinic acetylcholine receptor

Muscarinic acetylcholine receptoris NOT an ion channel, but a G-protein coupled receptor

Potassium channel

Synport/antiport proteins

Glucose transporter

Hormones and growth factors

Oxytocin

Insulin

Epidermal growth factor

Insulin-like growth factor

Receptors

Receptors with enzyme activity are in the enzymes section.

Receptors that are ion channels are in the ion channel section.

Transmembrane receptors

G-protein-coupled receptor

Rhodopsin

Intracellular receptors

Estrogen receptor

DNA-binding protein

Histones

Transcription regulation

CI protein %

Transcription regulatory proteins that are receptors are in the receptors section.

C-myc	FOXP2
MyoD	FOXP3
	P53

Immune system proteins

Immunoglobins

T cell receptor

Major histocompatibility antigens

Nutrient storage/transport

Ferritin

Chaperone proteins

GroEL %

Enzymes

Complexes with multiple components including proteins

Spliceosome

Ribonucleoprotein (generic)

Signal recognition particle

Nucleosome

PROTEIN BIOSYNTHESIS

Protein synthesis is the process in which cells build proteins. The term is sometimes used to refer only to protein translation but more often it refers to a multi-step process, beginning with amino acid synthesis and transcription which are then used for translation. Protein biosynthesis, although very similar, is different for prokaryotes and eukaryotes.

Amino acids are the monomers which are polymerized to produce proteins. Amino acid synthesis is the set of biochemical processes (metabolic pathways) which build the amino acids from carbon sources like glucose. Not all amino acids may be synthesised by every organism, for example adult humans have to obtain 8 of the 20 amino acids from their diet.

Transcription

Transcription is the process by which an mRNA template, encoding the sequence of the protein in the form of a trinucleotide code, is transcribed from the genome to provide a template for translation. Transcription copies the template from one strand of the DNA double helix, called the template strand.

Transcription can be divided into 3 stages: Initiation, Elongation and Termination, each regulated by a large number of proteins such as transcription factors and coactivators that ensure the correct gene is transcribed in response to appropriate signals.

The DNA strand is read in the 3′ to 5′ direction and the mRNA is transcribed in the 5′ to 3′ direction by the RNA polymerase.

Translation

The synthesis of proteins is known as translation. Translation occurs in the cytoplasm where the ribosomes are located. Ribosomes are made of a small and large subunit which surrounds the mRNA. In translation, messenger RNA (mRNA) is decoded to produce a specific polypeptide according to the rules specified by the genetic code. This uses an mRNA sequence as a template to guide the synthesis of a chain of amino acids that form a protein. Translation is necessarily preceded by transcription. Translation proceeds in four phases: activation, initiation, elongation and termination (all describing the growth of the amino acid chain, or polypeptide that is the product of translation).

In activation, the correct amino acid (AA) is joined to the correct transfer RNA (tRNA). While this is not technically a step in translation, it is required for translation to proceed. The AA is joined by its carboxyl group to the 3′ OH of the tRNA by an ester bond. When the tRNA has an amino acid linked to it, it is termed "charged". Initiation involves the small subunit of the ribosome binding to 5′ end of mRNA with the help of initiation factors (IF), other proteins that assist the process. Elongation occurs when the next aminoacyl-tRNA (charged tRNA) in line binds to the ribosome along with GTP and an elongation factor. Termination of the polypeptide happens when the A site of the ribosome faces a stop codon (UAA, UAG, or UGA). When this happens, no tRNA can recognize it, but releasing factor can recognize nonsense codons and causes the release of the polypeptide chain. The capacity of disabling or inhibiting translation in protein biosynthesis is used by antibiotics such as: anisomycin, cycloheximide, chloramphenicol, tetracycline, streptomycin, erythromycin, puromycin etc.

EVENTS FOLLOWING PROTEIN TRANSLATION

The events following biosynthesis include post-translational modification and protein folding. During and after synthesis, polypeptide chains often fold to assume, so called, native secondary and tertiary structures. This is known as protein folding.

Many proteins undergo post-translational modification. This may include the formation of disulfide bridges or attachment of any of a number of biochemical functional groups, such as acetate, phosphate, various lipids and carbohydrates. Enzymes may also remove one or more amino acids from the leading (amino) end of the polypeptide chain, leaving a protein consisting of two polypeptide chains connected by disulfide bonds.

Protein Structure

The order of amino acids in a protein molecule is genetically determined. This primary sequence of amino acids must contain all the information required for the protein to assume its correct three-dimensional structure. The primary structure is composed of amino acids linked together in what are termed peptide bonds. At first glance these appear to contain only single bonds and free rotation between all such atoms would be expected.

Measurements of bond angles and lengths of peptide bonds suggests however, that the C = O bond of the carbonyl group is longer than would be expected for such a bond and that the C - N bond is shorter than would be expected. This has led to the concept of the hybrid bonding situation as depicted in fig. 7.1.

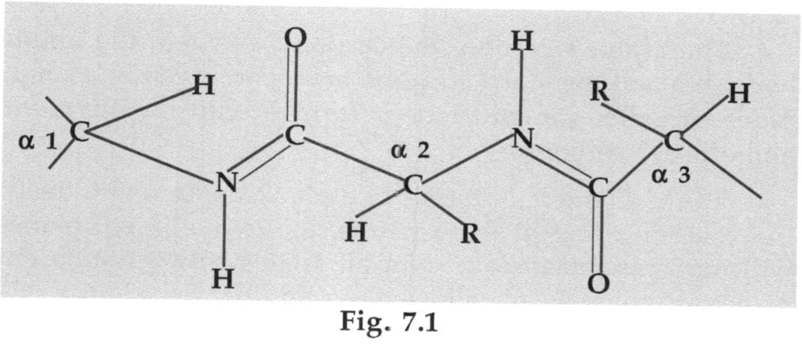

Fig. 7.1

The dotted lines represent the sharing of the electrons that normally would be expected to be found in the double bond. The result is that neither bond behaves as though it were a single or a double bond but rather has intermediate properties. One of the properties it obtains is the lack of rotation between the bonded atoms. This results in the situation as shown in fig. 7.2.

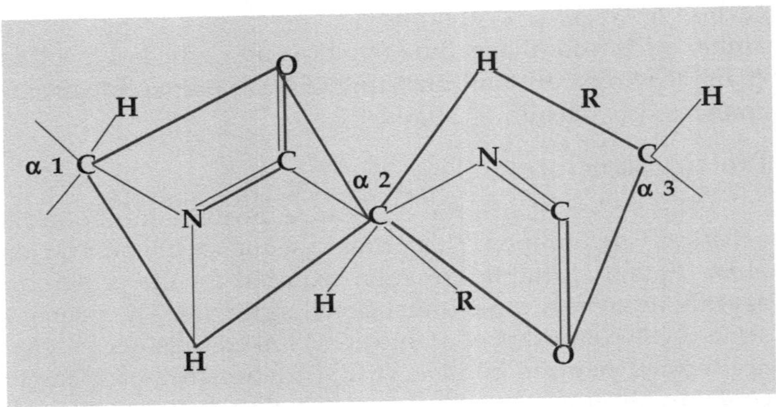

Fig. 7.2

In this structure there is no rotation about the bond:

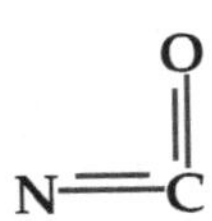

This results in the formation of a series of planes as indicated by the dotted lines in Fig. 7.2.

The alpha 1 carbon, the carbonyl oxygen, the amide hydrogen and the alpha 2 carbon are all arranged in a single plane. Another similar plane is formed with the alpha a 2 and alpha 3 carbons.

The C-C and C-N bonds of alpha 2 C can rotate freely. .As rotation occur at these points, the two adjacent planes will move as intact units. Not all angles between adjacent planes are energetically allowed. Angles that force bulky side chains to come into close contact or for groups with like charges to approach are not allowed.

Scientists utilized space filling models and computer simulation to calculate the energies of various combinations of planer angles. When such calculations were made, it was found that most angles yielded areas of high energy and were not allowed. There were, however, areas that yielded minimal values and these angles were the ones that would be expected to be found in protein molecules.

Data obtained from x-ray diffraction of proteins indicates that the predicted angles agreed very well with those observed. Only the amino acid glycine , which contains a hydrogen as an R group, showed major deviation from the predicted angles.

These allowed-angles at areas of low energy correspond to structures that have been observed repeatedly in proteins. This next level of order has been termed secondary structure.

Secondary Structure

Alpha Helix

In the early 1950's Pauling and Corey examined the bond lengths and angles of the atoms in amino acids in crystals. They then attempted to devise a repeating structure that would maintain these lengths and also maximize hydrogen bonding. The structure they suggested was a helix that contained 3.6 amino acid residues per turn.

Each peptide can be considered as a plane that is tangent to the axis of the helix. There are 100 degrees of rotation from one amino acid to the next which results in a helix with 3.6 amino acids per turn. Each peptide group; is hydrogen bonded to the third peptide along the chain in either direction. This is a very compact structure that does not have room for water or other small molecules in the interior. A protein that was comprised of only alpha-helix would be a rigid, long, narrow rod. Proteins vary greatly in a helix content from a low of less than 5% to a high of greater than 80%. The first protein to be examined by high resolution x-ray diffraction was myoglobin. About 80% of the amino acid residues in myoglobin were found in one of its 8 helical segments. Most proteins do not contain this much helical structure.

While there is no room in the interior of the helix for even small molecules, interactions of amino acid side chains at its surface are quite common. The residues comprising an alpha helix may be either hydrophobic or hydrophilic and the location of the helix will dictate which type of residue is found. Often a helix is located at the surface of a protein with one side exposed to the solvent and the other side making contact with other portions of the protein molecule. This results in a situation where all hydrophobic groups are found on one side of a helix with only hydrophilic groups on the other side.

The helical structure also requires that there be favourable interactions between at least three consecutive amino acid residues. this means that a helix doesn't begin to form easily, but once it is formed it is a fairly stable structure. The hydrogen bonds between atoms within the helix are generally not exposed to full contact with the solvent. This lack of solvent interaction causes these hydrogen bonds to be more stable than those observed in small compounds that are more fully hydrated.

To help visualize a helix, the following show a segment of a protein composed of two sections of alpha helix. The first view is a ball and stick representation of the amino acids. The dotted lines indicate hydrogen bonds. The helix is difficult to discern from this representation. The next view is a wire frame representation of the same portion of the molecule. With the amino acids represented in less space, the helical structures are easier to see. The final view is a cartoon representation of the helical structure of the same protein fragment. It may help you to alternate the views and attempt to become better at visualizing the helix.

Beta-Structure

If a chain of amino acids is drawn in a linear extended conformation, the R groups will fall alternately above and below the plain of the peptide bonds. If another chain of extended amino acids is brought near the first chain, it is a simple matter to line up the chain so as to maximize hydrogen bonding. This can be done whether the chains have the same N to C sense (parallel) or not (anti parallel).

Pauling and Corey first proposed the proper hydrogen bonding scheme for parallel and anti-parallel beta structure. The hydrogen bonds are evenly spaced in parallel sheets, but show a more irregular spacing in anti parallel sheets. In both cases, the number of hydrogen bonds formed is maximal. The number of strands involved in beta structure can range from 2 to more than 10. anti parallel sheets are the only ones generally involving only two strands, while both parallel and anti-parallel strands of five or more chains are quite common. Some sheets are mixed containing strands that are bonded to a parallel strand on one side and an anti parallel one on the other. The strands making up the beta structure may be derived from a single chain with no intervening structure or they may be separated by areas of helical structure. In some cases the beta structure may involve amino acids from two or more separate polypeptide chains.

While the R groups of adjacent amino acids appear on opposite sides of the chain, the groups of the separate chains that comprise beta structure are in close proximity. The types of forces describes the interaction between these R groups and add stability to the B structures. These forces are stronger in portions of the strands that have been removed from intimate contact with water.

The R groups on one side of a chain tend to be either all hydrophilic or all hydrophobic in anti parallel sheets. Thus, one side of the strand will either favor exposure to the solvent or to other chains that contain hydrophobic regions. In parallel sheets, the R groups tend to be more uniformly hydrophobic and these strands are only rarely exposed to the solvent. Similar to the structures for alpha-helix, the following show beta-structure in either a ball and stick, wire frame and cartoon form.

Large numbers of anti-parallel sheets may associate into structures described as barrels. These structures are composed of from 5 to 13 separate strands. The core regions of these barrels are very hydrophobic. Such structures have been identified in a number of proteins and have been reported to have about the same cross sectional area regardless of the number of strands they are composed of. The conditions required for the formation of beta structure are not as rigid as for the formation of alpha helix. In many cases a couple of amino acids having an extended structure can be hydrogen bonded to another couple of amino acids that are separated by a large number of intervening amino acids. Such interactions should be considered as beta structure. The following show beta barrels in either a ball and stick, wire frame and cartoon form.

Beta Bends

When a chain folds back on itself to form an anti parallel beta sheet, the conformation of the amino acids in the turn portion are generally in one of two conformations. The structures shown are the classic beta bends. Many variations of these have been found and some authors suggest there are up to ten types of turns with variations for each type.

The original beta bends were recognized to be stabilized by hydrogen bonding within the four amino acids composing the bends. As similar structures have been located in additional proteins, it has been observed that almost half of them are stable without the occurrence of any hydrogen bonding. In these cases, just the normal energy constraints of the bond angles lead to stable structures.

Beta bends are important to protein structure. These small structures direct the main chains of proteins into directions that allow for proper interactions. Depending on the criteria for defining beta bends, they have been estimated to consist of from 20 to 45% of the total structure of all proteins.

At one time it was popular to refer to all secondary structure of proteins that was not alpha-helix or beta sheet as random coil. This term gives the unfortunate connotation of a random, dynamic structure for much of the protein. What is really meant, is that no readily apparent repeating structure is present. The fact that proteins form well-defined crystals and that sharp x-ray diffraction patterns can be obtained form these crystals, suggests that essentially all of the molecules of a given type of protein are in the same three-dimensional conformation. Thus random should, in this case, be used to suggest no readily apparent repeating structure rather than a truly random location of the amino acid residues.

Beta bends were the first non-repeating, yet organized structures that have been recognized in proteins. Their greatest contribution to the structure of proteins may be their direction of protein folding. It remains to be seen if other regular non-repeating structures will be recognized in proteins.

Tertiary Structure

The final three dimensional structure a protein assumes is called its tertiary structure. This level of structure defines the location of each amino acid of the protein in three-dimensional space. Tertiary structure may be considered as being the same as the conformation of the protein. With few exceptions proteins are not long extended structures, but have dimensions that are not too different from spheres or ovoids. This suggest that once secondary structures have formed the molecules fold into relatively compact structures.

The specific tertiary structure assumed by a protein can have considerable impact on the properties of the molecule. The protein folds in such a way as to remove as many hydrophobic groups as is possible from contact with the aqueous phase. The final conformation should also attempt to maximize favorable interactions between different portions of the molecule. This usually results in a molecule having a very compact interior. The hydrophobic groups are associated away from the water and are able to interact due to London forces. the interior of the molecule is usually devoid of water molecules or of charged amino acid residues. The energy required to over come the interactions of charged groups with water that would be necessary for their insertion into the protein interior is generally not available. When a protein does find the necessary energy to bury a charged group or even a dipole,the buried group usually can be shown to perform some specific function necessary to the functionality of the protein.

While the protein maximizes interactions between its constituent amino acids it will also optimize the number of interactions with the solvent. To a large extent the number and strength of these interactions will determine the solubility characteristics of the protein. It should be noted that the specific nature of the interactions that occur and thus the conformation of the protein are greatly dependent upon the environment. Changes in temperature, ionic strength, dielectric constant, pH, etc. would be expected to have affects on the structure of the protein. These changes may be very subtle or of great consequence to the structure and function of the molecule. Whenever the conformation of a protein is discussed the conditions must be specified so that others will be able to reproduce the observations.

The small protein lysozyme, molecular weight about 14,000, can be used to help visualize the tertiary structure of proteins. The first view of lysozyme is a space filling view. No evidence of secondary or tertiary structure is evident from this view. Removal of the depth of the atoms gievs the wire frame view. Some hydrogen bonds can no be seen as dots. The colour scheme for this representation has changed. Alpha helical structures appear as megenta, beta structures are yellow, turns are light blue and all other structures are white. This color scheme will be used in all subsequent representations of the lysozyme molecule. The color clues make visulization of the secondary features a little easier. We can also see how the secondary structes are arranged into tertiary structure. A back bone structure makes the visualization even easier. The hydrogen bonds are much clearer and the tertiary structure of the protein is evident. The final view is a cartoon representation of the tertiary structure.

A much larger molecule carboxypeptidase A, molecular weight about 94,000, is shown in the ball and stick, back bone and cartoon representations. As the complexity of the molecule increases, visualization of the tertiary strcuture becomes more difficult. As the figures indicate, the number of tertiary interactions also increase with size and complexity.

Quaternary Structures

Many protein molecules tend to associate in well-defined structures. Such associations are termed quaternary structures. These structures are often caused by the addition of small molecules or by slight changes in the structure of the individual molecules. Many enzymes, for instance, can be polymerized or depolymerized by the action of phosphatases or kinases. The addition or removal of a phosphate group from a protein molecule can greatly change its tendency to form associated structures.

In many cases an organism can rapidly change the activity of an enzyme by such modification of its quaternary structure. These modifications can be accomplished very rapidly and are readily reversible. This allows for rapid control of enzyme activity.

Many proteins of importance in food systems exhibit quaternary structure. Soy globulins, casein and actomyosin are just a few examples of such proteins. When these proteins are discussed in later chapters, the importance of quaternary structure to their functional properties will be discussed.

Protein Denaturation

Protein denaturation is commonly defined as any non-covalent change in the structure of a protein. This change may alter the secondary, tertiary or quaternary structure of the molecules. When using this definition it should be noted that what constitutes denaturation is largely dependent upon the method utilized to observe the protein molecule. Some methods can detect very slight changes in structure while other require rather large alterations in structure before changes are observed.

Loss of Solubility

Changes in solubility might be evident in simple buffers or they might exhibit themselves only after exposure to other conditions, e.g. 0.25M ammonium sulfate. Proteins vary greatly in their resistance to insolubilization by a variety of procedures and some proteins that are very important in foods are insoluble in their native state. The loss of solubility is only one of the last stages in a series of changes in structure that must have occurred. As such, this is a rather crude measure of protein denaturation.

In another sense however, the loss of solubility can be related to the loss of a great number of desirable characteristics of the protein. In many cases in food systems, most structural changes other than loss of solubility are unimportant and the role of many process designs and food additives is to maintain protein solubility.

When more sophisticated techniques are utilized many changes in protein structure that eventually result in a loss of solubility can be detected. In these cases the loss of solubility is more properly regarded as an effect of denaturation rather than as a measure of denaturation. To a consumer or a product development scientist who only observes that feathering occurs when some products are utilized to whiten coffee, loss of solubility, however, is the only event that matters. In the rest of this chapter, loss of solubility will be considered as an effect of denaturation.

Increased Proteolysis

Most native proteins are quite resistant to the action of proteolytic enzymes. During digestion, proteins are exposed to extremes of pH to alter their structures in such a way as to expose the proper groups to enzyme molecules. For some time, it has been known that a variety of procedures that alter protein's structures make them more susceptible to proteolysis. The rate and extent of proteolysis can be utilized as an indictor of protein denaturation. In many cases, increases in proteolysis, like decreases in solubility, are the result of many changes in protein structure. In a series of experiments on ribonuclease, Burgess and Scheraga exposed this protein to a variety of combinations of pH and temperature. The molecule was then mixed with one of three different proteases. Under conditions of mild denaturation, they were able to observe which portions of the molecule were made susceptible to proteolysis first. Increasingly harsh treatments exposed other portions of the molecule to the action of the proteases. From these observations and a knowledge of the tertiary structure of the molecule, they were able to hypothesize a pathway for the thermal denaturation of ribonuclease. This pathway was assumed to be the reverse of the pathway for protein folding, but there was no evidence for this to be the case.

Loss of Biological Activity

For those proteins that are enzymes, denaturation can be defined as the loss of enough structure to render the enzyme inactive. Changes in the rate of the reaction, the affinity for substrate, pH optimum, temperature optimum, specificity of reaction, etc., may be affected by denaturation of enzyme molecules. Loss of enzymatic activity can be a very sensitive measure of denaturation as some assay procedures are capable of detecting very low levels of product. In some cases the loss of activity can be shown to occur only after some other changes in structure can be observed by other procedures.

There may technically, then be denaturation of the protein before loss of activity occurs. Enzymes are extremely important in the processing and preparing of food products. Processors may variously want to encourage or inhibit the activity of selected enzymes. In these cases, losses of activity may well be the only index of protein denaturation that are of interest. A number of protein molecules may exhibit biological activities that are not enzymatic in nature. Antibodies for instance are capable of interacting with specific antigen molecules. Other proteins, like hemoglobin, may function as carriers while some, eg. ferritin, may function in the storage of specific components. The loss of any of these activities can be measured as protein denaturation.

Tritium-Hydrogen Exchange

When compounds that contain tritium are placed in water they will rapidly exchange the tritium for normal hydrogen if the groups containing the tritium are exposed to the water. Tritium may be incorporated into proteins by a number of procedures. Probably the most common in exchange experiments involves the unfolding of the protein molecule in a medium where all of the water has been replaced by tritium oxide. When the protein is removed to a normal aqueous environment, three classes of tritium are often observed. Any tritium that is on the surface of the molecule along with any other that is not necessarily always on the surface, but that comes into contact with the surface under the conditions of study, will rapidly be lost from the molecule.

A second class of tritium molecules will be lost only when conditions that lead to partial protein unfolding occur. These are the class that can be utilized to monitor the rate and extent of denaturation. There may also exist a set of tritium molecules that are located in positions that are accessible to solvent only when the protein molecule is completely unfolded. The second group of tritium atoms do not exchange with the solvent because they are not exposed to the water. Such molecules must be located on the interior of the protein. If denaturation results in unfolding of the molecule and exposure of previously buried tritium groups to the solvent, exchange will occur. This procedure has been utilized quite extensively to study the mechanisms of stabilization of protein structure by small molecules.

Spectroscpic Procedures

A variety of procedures have been developed that measure the interaction of electromagnetic radiation with molecules. Some of these procedures have proven to be very useful in the study of protein denaturation. One such procedure is ultraviolet adsorption spectroscopy. This simply measures the wavelength of and the amount of ultraviolet radiation absorbed by a molecule. In proteins, both the wavelength and extent of absorption depend on the amino acids present and on their physical environments. There are a large number of such groups in a protein molecule and thus its U.V. spectrum quite often lacks detail.

Under some circumstances however, these groups can absorb at a low wavelength, generally in the U.V., and then emit light at a larger wavelength. This process is known as fluores/cence and is quite sensitive to the environment of the groups involved. Both ultraviolet and fluorescence spectroscopy have been utilized to follow changes in the environments of various groups within protein molecules. Such changes in environment reflect changes in protein structure and thus denaturation. The interaction of polarized light with protein can be measured by the techniques of circular dichroism and optical rotatory dispersion.

These methods yield an indication of the extent of repeating structures present in protein and are generally utilized to give estimates of the amount of secondary structure present, eg. alpha-helix, beat sheet or coil. While these procedures do not yield very precise estimates of the exact secondary structure of proteins, they are very useful for observing changes. These methods are very sensitive and rather small changes in structure can be detected.

Causes of Protein Denaturation

Changes in the structure of proteins can be caused by a variety of factors. Some of these are encountered frequently while others are more of theoretical interests. Some of the important mechanisms of protein denaturation to food scientists will be discussed.

Thermal Denaturation

When proteins are exposed to increasing temperature, losses of solubility or enzymatic activity occurs over a fairly narrow range. Depending upon the protein studied and the severity of the heating, these changes may or may not be reversible. As the temperature is increased, a number of bonds in the protein molecule are weakened. The first affected are the long range interactions that are necessary for the presence of tertiary structure. As these bonds are first weakened and are broken, the protein obtains a more flexible structure and the groups are exposed to solvent. If heating ceases at this stage the protein should be able to readily refold to the native structure. As heating continues, some of the cooperative hydrogen bonds that stabilize helical structure will begin to break.

As these bonds are broken, water can interact with and form new hydrogen bonds with the amide nitrogen and carbonyl oxygens of the peptide bonds. The presence of water further weakens nearby hydrogen bonds by causing an increase in the effective dielectric constant near them. As the helical structure is broken, hydrophobic groups are exposed to the solvent. The effect of exposure of new hydrogen bonding groups and of hydrophobic groups is to increase the amount of water bound by the protein molecules. The unfolding that occurs increase the hydrodynamic radius of the molecule causing the viscosity of the solution to increase. The net result will be an attempt by the protein to minimize its free energy by burying as many hydrophobic groups while exposing as many polar groups as possible to the solvent. While this is analogous to what occurred when the protein folded originally, it is happening at a much higher temperature.

This greatly weakens the short range interaction that initially direct protein folding and the structures that occur will often be vastly different from the native protein. Upon cooling, the structures obtained by the aggregated proteins may not be those of lowest possible free energy, but kinetic barriers will prevent them from returning to the native format. Any attempt to obtain the native structure would first require that the hydrophobic bonds that caused the aggregation be broken. This would be energetically unfavorable and highly unlikely. Only when all the intermolecular hydrophobic bonds were broken, could the protein begin to refold as directed by the energy of short range interactions.

The exposure of this large number of hydrophobic groups to the solvent, however, presents a large energy barrier that make such a refolding kinetically unlikely. Exposure of most proteins to high temperatures results in irreversible denaturation. Some proteins, like caseins, however, contain little if any secondary structure and have managed to remove their hydrophobic groups from contact with the solvent without the need for extensive structure.

This lack of secondary structure causes these proteins to be extremely resistant to thermal denaturation. The increased water binding noted in the early stages of denaturation may be retained following hydrophobic aggregations. The loss of solubility that occurs will greatly reduce the viscosity to a level below that of the native proteins. The effect of thermal denaturation on the functional properties of specific proteins will be discussed in subsequent chapters.

pH Denaturation

Most proteins at physiological pH are above their isoelectric points and have a net negative charge. When the pH is adjusted to the isoelectric point of the protein, its net charge will be zero. Charge repulsions of similar molecules will be at minimum and many proteins will precipitate. Even for proteins that remain in solution at their isoelectric points, this is usually the pH of minimum solubility. If the pH is lowered far below the isoelectric point, the protein will lose its negative and contain only positive charges. The like charges will repel each other and prevent the protein from aggregating as readily.

In areas of large charge density, the intramolecular repulsion may be great enough to cause unfolding of the protein. This will have an effect similar to that of mild heat treatment on the protein structure. In some cases the unfolding may be extensive enough to expose hydrophobic groups and cause irreversible aggregation. Until this occurs such unfolding will be largely reversible. Some proteins contain acid labile groups and even relatively mild acid treatment may cause irreversible loss of function. This generally results from the breaking of specific covalent bonds and thus should be considered separately from denaturation. Exposure to strong enough acid at elevated temperatures will first release amide nitrogen from glutamine and asparagine groups and eventually lead to hydrolysis of peptide bonds. The effects of high pH are analogous to those of low pH.

The proteins obtain a large negative charge which can cause unfolding and even aggregation. The use of high pH to solubilize and alter protein structure is very important to the formation of fibers from proteins of plant origin. A number of reactions can cause chemical modification of proteins at alkaline pH's that are commonly encountered in protein processing. Many of these involve cysteine residues. Perhaps the most important are the base catalyzed beta eliminations of sulfur to yield dehydroalanine which can react with lysine to form lysinoalanine. This results in a loss of nutritive value of the protein and the products of the reaction may be toxic. Exposure of protein molecules to high pH should be minimized as much as is possible. Exposure to very high pH at elevated temperatures results in alkaline hydrolysis of peptide bonds.

Changes in Dielectric Constant

The addition of a solvent that is miscible with water, but that is less polar will lower the dielectric constant of the system. This will tend to increase the strength of all electrostatic interactions between molecules that were in contact with water. Many of the protein hydrogen bonds are effectively removed from the solvent and will not be affected. The presence of the less polar solvent will also have the effect of weakening the hydrophobic bonds of the proteins. These bonds depend upon an increase in the order of water when they are broken for their existence. As there is less water in the system, this becomes less important and at some level of replacement, these groups are at a lower energy level when in contact with the solvent. The structure of the protein will be changed and hence, it will be denatured. The reversibility of the process depends to a large extent on the nature of the non-polar solvent, the extent of unfolding the temperature of the system and the rate of solvent removal.

When large amounts of the solvent are present, the protein will be largely unfolded with extensive exposure of the hydrophobic groups. If the protein could be instantaneously transferred to pure water at room temperature, the protein would most likely aggregate and precipitate. The sudden exposure of the hydrophobic groups to water would cause them to try to remove themselves from the aqueous phase as soon as possible. Even before the short range interactions could redirect the folding of the protein aggregation would occur. If the solvent exchange were slow, there would be a better chance that the hydrophobic groups would be able to return to the interior of the molecule and prevent aggregation.

If the exchange occurred at low temperatures, the chances of regaining the native structure would be even better. At low temperatures, the hydrophobic groups may in part be stable in the aqueous phase or at least not as unstable. In this case, the removal of the solvent has little affect. When the temperature is subsequently increased, the normal course of protein refolding can occur. Solvent precipitation is often utilized as a means of purifying and concentrating enzymes. It is extremely important that both the solvent and the protein solution be cold when they are mixed and that the subsequent removal of the solvent be performed at reduced temperature. This helps to insure the recovery of enzyme activity.

Denaturation at Interfaces

When proteins are exposed to either liquid-air or liquid-liquid interfaces, denaturation can occur. As a liquid-liquid interface, the protein comes into contact with a hydrophobic environment. If allowed to remain at this interface for a period of time proteins will tend to unfold and place as many of their hydrophobic groups as possible in the non-aqueous layer while maintaining as much charge as possible in the water layer. To understand why protein unfold at hydrophobic interfaces, it must be realized that the tertiary structure of a protein is not rigid.

There are continued fluctuations about an average configuration. Any change in conformation that yields a higher energy state will spontaneously go back to the state of lowest energy. As a part of this process, hydrophobic groups will occasionally be positioned so that they have increased contact with the aqueous phase. When this occurs, these groups will assume the configuration of lowest free energy and will be removed from the water. If a hydrophobic group is exposed while a protein is in contact with a polar solvent, these groups will find a state of lower energy exists if they enter into the solvent phase. This will continue to occur until random fluctuations in protein structure can no longer yield a configuration of lower free energy. The amount of unfolding that occurs at such an interface will depend on how rigid the three-dimensional protein structure is an on the number and location of hydrophobic groups in the molecule.

A flexible, non-crosslinked protein will be able to unfold easier than will a highly structured and crosslinked one. If energy is applied to cause shear, the process will be accelerated. The shear can cause the protein to unfold, thus exposing its hydrophobic groups to the nonaqueous phase. It can also increase the interfacial area between the two phases and allow more proteins to come into contact with the nonaqueous phase. This unfolding is essentially non-reversible because of the large energy barriers. Even if the phases should separate and the protein is forced into the aqueous phase the protein will not regain its original structure. Rather an association of hydrophobic groups will cause the protein to aggregate.

The same forces are in operation when a protein migrates to a liquid-air interface. Hydrophobic groups tend to associate in the air and the protein unfolds. The presence of shear causes to help unfold the protein and to introduce more air into the solution. Both of these effects can be minimized by keeping the temperature low (to weaken hydrophobic bonds) and by minimizing the interfacial area. If the interface is limited, then only a small amount of protein will be able to denature. The presence of this denatured protein will serve as a barrier to further denaturation. Proteins are often utilized in food products to stabilize emulsions or to incorporate air. These cases will be examined in more detail when emulsions and foams are discussed.

Ionic Strength

Proteins are usually more soluble in dilute salt solutions than in pure water. The salts are thought to associate with oppositely charge groups in the protein. This combination of charged groups bonds more water than do the charged groups alone and protein hydration is increased. With most proteins there is little change in solubility as more salt is added until some very high salt content is reached. At very high levels of salt there is a competition between the ions and the proteins for water of hydration. When the salt concentration is high enough, the proteins will be sufficiently dehydrated to lose solubility. Removal of the salt or dilution to a low enough concentration will usually result in the recovery of native structure.

The Effect of Protein Crosslinkers

The presence of groups that crosslink protein molecules will tend to lower the extent of protein denaturation. There are two main reasons that this is so. First, when proteins are crosslinked it is more difficult for them to unfold. As energy is added to the system and secondary bonds are weakened, the presence of crosslinkers will tend to maintain structure. This is especially true if the crosslinks are covalent as in the case of disulfide bonds. The more compact the molecule is and the greater the number of disulfide linkages present, the greater the stability of the protein. While secondary forces may be weakened and some bonds can be broken, the crosslinkers will tend to keep these groups in fairly close proximity. They also tend to prevent the exposure of large numbers of hydrophobic groups to the solvent.

When conditions are returned to the native state, there is now a much greater chance for the proper secondary interaction to occur and for the protein to assume the native configuration. A second effect has to do with the differences in entropy between the native and unfolded states. If a protein can be caused to assume a completely random coil conformation, there will be a large increase in entropy compared to the native structure. This entropy must be overcome if the protein is to refold into a native conformation. When crosslinking groups are present, a completely random coil conformation can not be assumed. These groups introduce order into the structure and there is a considerable loss in the amount of disorder that can be achieved in the most denatured state. Because of this, the entropy change between the native and denatured state is not nearly as great and there will be less of a driving force for denaturation.

If the crosslinking groups are broken before denaturation and thus allowed to randomly form after denaturation, no stability will be added to the protein by the pressure of these groups. Functionality has been defined as: "any property of a food or food ingredient, except its nutritional ones, that affects its utilization." For proteins then, there must be a large number of functions and functional properties listed in Table 7.1 are some of the most important ones to consider when discussing proteins.

- Functions of proteins in foods
- Flavor Dough Formation
- Binding Fiber Spinning
- Water Binding Thermal Extrusion
- Viscosity Emulsification
- Gelation Foam Formation

A protein manifests functionality by interacting with other compnents within the food system. These interactions may involve solvent molecules, solute molecules, other protein molecules or substances that are dispersed in the solvent such as oil or air.

In order to describe the forces involved in these interactions, it is essential that the forces and energies involved in the achievement and maintenance of native protein structure be described. While a complete discussion of the forces involved is beyond the scope of this chapter, some observations on the nature of protein structure will be useful. Proteins exist in the lowest kinetically attainable state of free energy. The free energy of the protein may not be the global minimum, but it will be the lowest that the protein can achieve in a reasonable period of time. Protein structure is highly dependent upon the environment and the protein will assume different conformation as the environmental conditions change. Factors of importance include pH, temperature, dielectric constant, ionic strength and the presence of other molecules including air, fat, denaturants, etc.

One of the main ways that proteins lower their free energy involves the removal the removal of hydrophobic groups from the aqueous environment. This may provide the greatest single decrease in free energy of all the types of binding that occur within proteins. The strength of hydrophobic binding is, however, very sensitive to changes in temperature and dielectric constant and thus changes in these parameters can have large influences on protein structure. Protein molecules may contain crosslinks of a non-covalent, e.g. salt bridges or a covalent, eg. disulfide bonds, nature. These crosslinks lower the conformational entropy of the molecule which must be compensated for by a decrease in binding energy. The presence of crosslinks adds greatly to the stability of the native protein structure and makes the molecules resistant to unfolding or denaturation. For example, simple unfolding is inhibited sterically by the presence of crosslinking because portions of the molecules are held in place by the crosslinks.

Denaturation is also less likely because one of the driving forces of denaturation, an increase in conformational entropy is greatly reduced. In a non-crosslinked protein, if unfolding to a random coil structure can be induced, there is a very large gain in the number of conformations the molecule can assume. This gain in conformational entropy is a large driving force for the maintenance of the denatured state when the denaturing agents are removed. In contrast, a highly crosslinked protein cannot assume the same degree of random conformations and thus the increase in entropy is much less.

This helps explain why molecules that contain large numbers of disulfide bonds are often resistant to denaturation. The structures attained by proteins are not rigid, but are very dynamic. There is rotational freedom about many of the bonds within the protein molecule and the entropy gain of this freedom lowers the total free energy of the native structure. There are also portions of the protein structure that are stabilized by rather weak secondary forces and these are often free to assume different conformations.

These alternate conformations lead to structures of higher free energy and thus are not stable or long lived. A protein may be envisioned as a dynamic entity that is constantly sampling a variety of structures. These new structures are usually only slightly different from the native conformation and almost always lead to a situation where the free energy of this system increases. The increase in free energy causes the protein to spontaneously refold into the state of lowest free energy. Thus, the native structure of a protein is not the only structure it can assume, but rather the one of lowest free energy and hence of greatest probability. Slight changes in the environment can cause alternate structures to be of lowest free energy and thus lead to protein denaturation.

In order for a protein to exhibit functionality, it must interact with other components of the food system. These interactions may often require that the protein be free to either move throughout the system or to alter its structure in such a way to allow interactions with other components.

In some cases the simple presence of other molecules in the protein solution will allow interaction to occur, but more commonly, the interactions require an input of energy into the system to insure adequate mixing. This energy may alter the physical nature of the molecules being mixed, eg. decrease in average fat globule size and also alter the conformation of the protein molecule.

Flavour

In order for a compound to have flavour it must either interact with one of the four basic taste receptors on the tongue (sweet, sour, bitter or salty) or it must be volatile enough to interact with odor receptors in the olfactory organ. Most proteins can do neither of and so they have little direct impact on flavor. While free proteins as such have little affect, they may contribute to food flavour through one of the following:

- bound molecules
- absorption
- break down products
- chemical reactions.

Protein Hydrophobicity

- Hydrophobic groups can form crosslinks in protein gels
- Excessive hydrophobicity can cause aggregation prior to proper crosslink formation
- In normal WPC, increased hydrophobicity increases gel strength

Emulsification

Emulsions are thermodynamically unstable mixtures of immiscible liquids. If energy is applied the systems may be dispersed, but increased surface energy causes the phases to coalesce unless an energy barrier to coalescence is established. The forces responsible for phase separation include:

- Phase Separation
- Lipid-lipid interactions are predominantly due to London forces.
- Water-Water interactions are predominantly due to H bonds.

Water-Lipid Interactions

- DG is positive
- DH is negative
- DS is negative

Factors Important to Protein Stabilized Emulsions

- Rate of diffusion
- Solubility
- Viscosity
- Protein Flexibility
- Net Charge
- Protein Hydrophobicity
- Protein Stabilized Emulsions

In order to form and stabilize an emulsion, a protein must:

- Diffuse to the interface
- Unfold
- Expose hydrophobic groups
- Interact with lipid
- Temperature
- Emulsion formation favored around 60 C

- Lower viscosity
- Favors hydrophobic interactions

Lower temperature decreases energy barrier to lipid-water interactions.

- Freezing can cause physical damage to the interface
- Diffusion
- Protein must diffuse to the interface
- Rate of diffusion affected by presence of salts
- Rate of diffusion affected by viscosity

Most studies indicate that diffusion from the bulk phase to the interface is rate limiting.

Emulsified droplets can be stabilized by the addition of molecules that are partially soluble in both phases. In foods a number of small emulsifier molecules can serve this function. Proteins capable of unfolding at the interface may also serve this function. Protein coats the lipid droplet and provides an energy barrier to particle association and phase separation.

Stoke's law:

$$v = \frac{2r^2 g \Delta p}{9\mu}$$

Where v equals the velocity of the fat globule, r is the radius of the fat globule, g is the force of gravity, Δp is the density difference between the two phases and μ is the viscosity of the continuous phase.

CHAPTER

8

Enzymes

Enzymes are biomolecules that catalyze (i.e., increase the rates of) chemical reactions Almost all enzymes are proteins. In enzymatic reactions, the molecules at the beginning of the process are called substrates, and the enzyme converts them into different molecules, the products. Almost all processes in a biological cell need enzymes to occur at significant rates. Since enzymes are selective for their substrates and speed up only a few reactions from among many possibilities, the set of enzymes made in a cell determines which metabolic pathways occur in that cell.

Like all catalysts, enzymes work by lowering the activation energy (E_a or $\Delta G^\ddagger$) for a reaction, thus dramatically increasing the rate of the reaction. Most enzyme reaction rates are millions of times faster than those of comparable un-catalyzed reactions. As with all catalysts, enzymes are not consumed by the reactions they catalyze, nor do they alter the equilibrium of these reactions. However, enzymes do differ from most other catalysts by being much more specific.

Enzymes are known to catalyze about 4,000 biochemical reactions. A few RNA molecules called ribozymes catalyze reactions, with an important example being some parts of the ribosome Synthetic molecules called artificial enzymes also display enzyme-like catalysis.

Enzyme activity can be affected by other molecules. Inhibitors are molecules that decrease enzyme activity; activators are molecules that increase activity. Many drugs and poisons are enzyme inhibitors. Activity is also affected by temperature, chemical environment (e.g., pH), and the concentration of substrate. Some enzymes are used commercially, for example, in the synthesis of antibiotics. In addition, some household products use enzymes to speed up biochemical reactions (e.g., enzymes in biological washing powders break down protein or fat stains on clothes; enzymes in meat tenderizers break down proteins, making the meat easier to chew).

Etymology and History

Eduard BuchnerAs early as the late 1700s and early 1800s, the digestion of meat by stomach secretions and the conversion of starch to sugars by plant extracts and saliva were known. However, the mechanism by which this occurred had not been identified

In the 19th century, when studying the fermentation of sugar to alcohol by yeast, Louis Pasteur came to the conclusion that this fermentation was catalyzed by a vital force contained within the yeast cells called "ferments", which were thought to function only within living organisms. He wrote that "alcoholic fermentation is an act correlated with the life and organization of the yeast cells, not with the death or putrefaction of the cells.

In 1878, German physiologist Wilhelm Kühne (1837-1900) first used the term 'enzyme', which comes from Greek, "in leaven", to describe this process. The word enzyme was used later to refer to nonliving substances such as pepsin, and the word ferment was used to refer to chemical activity produced by living organisms.

In 1897, Eduard Buchner began to study the ability of yeast extracts that lacked any living yeast cells to ferment sugar. In a series of experiments at the University of Berlin, he found that the sugar was fermented even when there were no living yeast cells in the mixture. He named the enzyme that brought about the fermentation of sucrose "zymase" In 1907, he received the Nobel Prize in Chemistry "for his biochemical research and his discovery of cell-free fermentation". Following Buchner's example, enzymes are usually named according to the reaction they carry out. Typically, to generate the name of an enzyme, the suffix -ase is added to the name of its substrate (e.g., lactase is the enzyme that cleaves lactose) or the type of reaction (e.g., DNA polymerase forms DNA polymers).

Having shown that enzymes could function outside a living cell, the next step was to determine their biochemical nature. Many early workers noted that enzymatic activity was associated with proteins, but several scientists (such as Nobel laureate Richard Willstätter) argued that proteins were merely carriers for the true enzymes and that proteins per se were incapable of catalysis. However, in 1926, James B. Sumner showed that the enzyme urease was a pure protein and crystallized it; Sumner did likewise for the enzyme catalase in 1937. The conclusion that pure proteins can be enzymes was definitively proved by Northrop and Stanley, who worked on the digestive enzymes pepsin (1930), trypsin and chymotrypsin. These three scientists were awarded the 1946 Nobel Prize in Chemistry.

This discovery that enzymes could be crystallized eventually allowed their structures to be solved by x-ray crystallography. This was first done for lysozyme, an enzyme found in tears, saliva and egg whites that digests the coating of some bacteria; the structure was solved by a group led by David Chilton Phillips and published in 1965 This high-resolution structure of lysozyme marked the beginning of the field of structural biology and the effort to understand how enzymes work at an atomic level of detail.

Structures and Mechanisms

Enzymes are generally globular proteins and range from just 62 amino acid residues in size, for the monomer of 4-oxalocrotonate tautomerase to over 2,500 residues in the animal fatty acid synthase. A small number of RNA-based biological catalysts exist, with the most common being the ribosome; these are referred to as either RNA-enzymes or ribozymes. The activities of enzymes are determined by their three-dimensional structure. However, although structure does determine function, predicting a novel enzyme's activity just from its structure is a very difficult problem that has not yet been solved.

Most enzymes are much larger than the substrates they act on, and only a small portion of the enzyme (around 3–4 amino acids) is directly involved in catalysis. The region that contains these catalytic residues, binds the substrate, and then carries out the reaction is known as the active site. Enzymes can also contain sites that bind cofactors, which are needed for catalysis. Some enzymes also have binding sites for small molecules, which are often direct or indirect products or substrates of the reaction catalyzed. This binding can serve to increase or decrease the enzyme's activity, providing a means for feedback regulation.

Like all proteins, enzymes are made as long, linear chains of amino acids that fold to produce a three-dimensional product. Each unique amino acid sequence produces a specific structure, which has unique properties. Individual protein chains may sometimes group together to form a protein complex. Most enzymes can be denatured—

that is, unfolded and inactivated—by heating or chemical denaturants, which disrupt the three-dimensional structure of the protein. Depending on the enzyme, denaturation may be reversible or irreversible.

Specificity

Enzymes are usually very specific as to which reactions they catalyze and the substrates that are involved in these reactions. Complementary shape, charge and hydrophilic/ hydrophobic characteristics of enzymes and substrates are responsible for this specificity. Enzymes can also show impressive levels of stereospecificity, regioselectivity and chemoselectivity.

Some of the enzymes showing the highest specificity and accuracy are involved in the copying and expression of the genome. These enzymes have "proof-reading" mechanisms. Here, an enzyme such as DNA polymerase catalyzes a reaction in a first step and then checks that the product is correct in a second step This two-step process results in average error rates of less than 1 error in 100 million reactions in high-fidelity mammalian polymerases Similar proofreading mechanisms are also found in RNA polymerase aminoacyl tRNA synthetases and ribosomes.

Some enzymes that produce secondary metabolites are described as promiscuous, as they can act on a relatively broad range of different substrates. It has been suggested that this broad substrate specificity is important for the evolution of new biosynthetic pathways.

"Lock and key" model

Enzymes are very specific, and it was suggested by Emil Fischer in 1894 that this was because both the enzyme and the substrate possess specific complementary geometric shapes that fit exactly into one another. This is often referred to as "the lock and key" model. However, while this model explains enzyme specificity, it fails to explain the stabilization of the transition state that enzymes achieve. The "lock and key" model has proven inaccurate, and the induced fit model is the most currently accepted enzyme-substrate-coenzyme figure.

Induced Fit Model

In 1958, Daniel Koshland suggested a modification to the lock and key model: since enzymes are rather flexible structures, the active site is continually reshaped by interactions with the substrate as the substrate interacts with the enzyme As a result, the substrate does not simply bind to a rigid active site; the amino acid side chains which make up the active site are moulded into the precise positions that enable the enzyme to perform its catalytic function. In some cases, such as glycosidases, the substrate molecule also changes shape slightly as it enters the active site. The active site continues to change until the substrate is completely bound, at which point the final shape and charge is determined.

Mechanisms

Enzymes can act in several ways, all of which lower $\Delta G^{\ddagger}$.

- Lowering the activation energy by creating an environment in which the transition state is stabilized (e.g. straining the shape of a substrate—by binding the transition-state conformation of the substrate/product molecules, the enzyme distorts the bound substrate(s) into their transition state form, thereby reducing the amount of energy required to complete the transition).
- Lowering the energy of the transition state, but without distorting the substrate, by creating an environment with the opposite charge distribution to that of the transition state.
- Providing an alternative pathway. For example, temporarily reacting with the substrate to form an

intermediate ES complex, which would be impossible in the absence of the enzyme.

- Reducing the reaction entropy change by bringing substrates together in the correct orientation to react. Considering ?H‡ alone overlooks this effect.

Interestingly, this entropic effect involves destabilization of the ground state, and its contribution to catalysis is relatively small.

Transition State Stabilization

The understanding of the origin of the reduction of $\Delta G^{\ddagger}$ requires one to find out how the enzymes can stabilize its transition state more than the transition state of the uncatalyzed reaction. Apparently, the most effective way for reaching large stabilization is the use of electrostatic effects, in particular, by having a relatively fixed polar environment that is oriented toward the charge distribution of the transition state. Such an environment does not exist in the uncatalyzed reaction in water.

Dynamics and Function

The internal dynamics of enzymes is connected to their mechanism of catalysis Internal dynamics are the movement of parts of the enzyme's structure, such as individual amino acid residues, a gr mportant in binding and releasing substrates and products, it is not clear if protein movements help to accelerate the chemical steps in enzymatic reactions These new insights also have implications in understanding allosteric effects and developing new drugs.

Allosteric Modulation

Allosteric enzymes change their structure in response to binding of effectors. Modulation can be direct, where the effector binds directly to binding sites in the enzyme, or indirect, where the effecor binds to other proteins or protein subunits that interact with the allosteric enzyme and thus influence catalytic activity.

Cofactors and Coenzymes

Co-factors

Some enzymes do not need any additional components to show full pounds (e.g., flavin and heme). Organic cofactors can be either prosthetic groups, which are tightly bound to an enzyme, or coenzymes, which are released from the enzyme's active site during the reaction. Coenzymes include NADH, NADPH and adenosine triphosphate. These molecules act to transfer chemical groups between enzymes.

An example of an enzyme that contains a cofactor is carbonic anhydrase, and is shown in the ribbon diagram above with a zinc cofactor bound as part of its active site.These tightly-bond molecules are usually found in the active site and are involved in catalysis. For example, flavin and heme cofactors are often involved in redox reactions.

Enzymes that require a cofactor but do not have one bound are called apoenzymes or apoproteins. An apoenzyme together with its cofactor(s) is called a holoenzyme (this is the active form). Most cofactors are not covalently attached to an enzyme, but are very tightly bound. However, organic prosthetic groups can be covalently bound (e.g., thiamine pyrophosphate in the enzyme pyruvate dehydrogenase). The term "holoenzyme" can also be applied to enzymes that contain multiple protein subunits, such as the DNA polymerases, here the holoenzyme is the complete complex containing all the subunits needed for activity.

Coenzymes

Coenzymes are small organic molecules that transport chemical groups from one enzyme to another. Some of these chemicals such as riboflavin, thiamine and folic acid are vitamins, this is when these compounds cannot be made in the body and must be acquired from the diet. The chemical groups carried include the hydride ion (H^-) carried by NAD or $NADP^+$, the acetyl group carried by coenzyme A, formyl, methenyl or methyl groups carried by folic acid and the methyl group carried by S-adenosylmethionine.

Since coenzymes are chemically changed as a consequence of enzyme action, it is useful to consider coenzymes to be a special class of substrates, or second substrates, which are common to many different enzymes. For example, about 700 enzymes are known to use the coenzyme NADH.

Coenzymes are usually regenerated and their concentrations maintained at a steady level inside the cell: for example, NADPH is regenerated through the pentose phosphate pathway and S-adenosylmethionine by methionine adenosyltransferase.

Thermodynamics

As all catalysts, enzymes do not alter the position of the chemical equilibrium of the reaction. Usually, in the presence of an enzyme, the reaction runs in the same direction as it would without the enzyme, just more quickly. However, in the absence of the enzyme, other possible uncatalyzed, "spontaneous" reactions might lead to different products, because in those conditions this different product is formed faster.

Furthermore, enzymes can couple two or more reactions, so that a thermodynamically favorable reaction can be used to "drive" a thermodynamically unfavorable one. For example, the hydrolysis of ATP is often used to drive other chemical reactions.

Enzymes catalyze the forward and backward reactions equally. They do not alter the equilibrium itself, but only the speed at which it is reached. For example, carbonic anhydrase catalyzes its reaction in either direction depending on the concentration of its reactants.

$$CO_2 + H_2O \xrightarrow{\text{Carbonic anhydrase}} H_2CO_3$$ (in tissue; high CO_2 concentration)

$$H_2CO_3 \xrightarrow{\text{Carbonic anhydrase}} CO_2 + H_2O$$ (in lungs; low CO_2 concentration)

Nevertheless, if the equilibrium is greatly displaced in one direction, that is, in a very exergonic reaction, the reaction is effectively irreversible. Under these conditions the enzyme will, in fact, only catalyze the reaction in the thermodynamically allowed direction.

Kinetics

Enzyme kinetics is the investigation of how enzymes bind substrates and turn them into products. The rate data used in kinetic analyses are obtained from enzyme assays.

In 1902 Victor Henri proposed a quantitative theory of enzyme kinetics, but his experimental data were not useful because the significance of the hydrogen ion concentration was not yet appreciated. After Peter Lauritz Sørensen had defined the logarithmic pH-scale and introduced the concept of buffering in 1909the German chemist Leonor Michaelis and his Canadian postdoc Maud Leonora Menten repeated Henri's experiments and confirmed his equation which is referred to as Henri-Michaelis-Menten kinetics (sometimes also Michaelis-Menten kinetics) Their work was further developed by G. E. Briggs and J. B. S. Haldane, who derived kinetic equations that are still widely used today.

The major contribution of Henri was to think of enzyme reactions in two stages. In the first, the substrate binds reversibly to the enzyme, forming the enzyme-substrate complex. This is sometimes called the Michaelis complex. The enzyme then catalyzes the chemical step in the reaction and releases the product.

Enzymes can catalyze up to several million reactions per second. For example, the reaction catalyzed by orotidine 5′-phosphate decarboxylase will consume half of its substrate in 78 million years if no enzyme is present. However, when the decarboxylase is added, the same process takes just 25 milliseconds Enzyme rates depend on solution conditions and substrate concentration. Conditions that denature the protein abolish enzyme activity, such as high temperatures, extremes of pH or high salt concentrations, while raising substrate concentration tends to increase activity. To find the maximum speed of an enzymatic reaction, the substrate concentration is increased until a constant rate of product formation is seen. This is shown in the saturation curve on the right. Saturation happens because, as substrate concentration increases, more and more of the free enzyme is converted into the substrate-bound ES form. At the maximum velocity (V_{max}) of the enzyme, all the enzyme active sites are bound to substrate, and the amount of ES complex is the same as the total amount of enzyme. However, V_{max} is only one kinetic constant of enzymes. The amount of substrate needed to achieve a given rate of reaction is also important. This is given by the Michaelis-Menten constant (K_m), which is the substrate concentration required for an enzyme to reach one-half its maximum velocity. Each enzyme has a characteristic K_m for a given substrate, and this can show how tight the binding of the substrate is to the enzyme. Another useful constant is k_{cat}, which is the number of substrate molecules handled by one active site per second.

The efficiency of an enzyme can be expressed in terms of k_{cat}/K_m. This is also called the specificity constant and incorporates the rate constants for all steps in the reaction. Because the specificity constant reflects both affinity and catalytic ability, it is useful for comparing different enzymes against each other, or the same enzyme with different substrates. The theoretical maximum for the specificity constant is called the diffusion limit and is about 10^8 to 10^9

(M^{-1} s^{-1}). At this point every collision of the enzyme with its substrate will result in catalysis, and the rate of product formation is not limited by the reaction rate but by the diffusion rate. Enzymes with this property are called catalytically perfect or kinetically perfect. Example of such enzymes are triose-phosphate isomerase, carbonic anhydrase, acetylcholinesterase, catalase, fumarase, ß-lactamase, and superoxide dismutase.

Michaelis-Menten kinetics relies on the law of mass action, which is derived from the assumptions of free diffusion and thermodynamically-driven random collision. However, many biochemical or cellular processes deviate significantly from these conditions, because of macromolecular crowding, phase-separation of the enzyme/ substrate/product, or one or two-dimensional molecular movement In these situations, a fractal Michaelis-Menten kinetics may be applied.

Some enzymes operate with kinetics which are faster than diffusion rates, which would seem to be impossible. Several mechanisms have been invoked to explain this phenomenon. Some proteins are believed to accelerate catalysis by drawing their substrate in and pre-orienting them by using dipolar electric fields. Other models invoke a quantum-mechanical tunneling explanation, whereby a proton or an electron can tunnel through activation barriers, although for proton tunneling this model remains somewhat controversia. Quantum tunneling for protons has been observed in tryptamine. This suggests that enzyme catalysis may be more accurately characterized as "through the barrier" rather than the traditional model, which requires substrates to go "over" a lowered energy barrier.

Inhibition

Enzyme reaction rates can be decreased by various types of enzyme inhibitors.

Competitive Inhibition

In competitive inhibition, the inhibitor and substrate compete for the enzyme (i.e., they can not bind at the same time). Often competitive inhibitors strongly resemble the real substrate of the enzyme. For example, methotrexate is a competitive inhibitor of the enzyme dihydrofolate reductase, which catalyzes the reduction of dihydrofolate to tetrahydrofolate. The similarity between the structures of folic acid and this drug are shown in the figure to the right bottom. Note that binding of the inhibitor need not be to the substrate binding site (as frequently stated), if binding of the inhibitor changes the conformation of the enzyme to prevent substrate binding and vice versa. In competitive inhibition the maximal velocity of the reaction is not changed, but higher substrate concentrations are required to reach a given velocity, increasing the apparent K_m.

Uncompetitive Inhibition

In uncompetitive inhibition the inhibitor can not bind to the free enzyme, but only to the ES-complex. The EIS-complex thus formed is enzymatically inactive. This type of inhibition is rare, but may occur in multimeric enzymes.

Non-competitive Inhibition

Non-competitive inhibitors can bind to the enzyme at the same time as the substrate, i.e. they never bind to the active site. Both the EI and EIS complexes are enzymatically inactive. Because the inhibitor can not be driven from the enzyme by higher substrate concentration (in contrast to competitive inhibition), the apparent V_{max} changes. But because the substrate can still bind to the enzyme, the K_m stays the same.

Mixed Inhibition

This type of inhibition resembles the non-competitive, except that the EIS-complex has residual enzymatic activity.

In many organisms inhibitors may act as part of a feedback mechanism. If an enzyme produces too much of one substance in the organism, that substance may act as an inhibitor for the enzyme at the beginning of the pathway that produces it, causing production of the substance to slow down or stop when there is sufficient amount. This is a form of negative feedback. Enzymes which are subject to this form of regulation are often multimeric and have allosteric binding sites for regulatory substances. Their substrate/velocity plots are not hyperbolar, but sigmoidal (S-shaped).

Irreversible inhibitors react with the enzyme and form a covalent adduct with the protein. The inactivation is irreversible. These compounds include eflornithine a drug used to treat the parasitic disease sleeping sickness Penicillin and Aspirin also act in this manner. With these drugs, the compound is bound in the active site and the enzyme then converts the inhibitor into an activated form that reacts irreversibly with one or more amino acid residues.

Uses of Inactivators

Inhibitors are often used as drugs, but they can also act as poisons. However, the difference between a drug and a poison is usually only a matter of amount, since most drugs are toxic at some level, as Paracelsus wrote, "In all things there is a poison, and there is nothing without a poison." Equally, antibiotics and other anti-infective drugs are just specific poisons that kill a pathogen but not its host.

An example of an inactivator being used as a drug is aspirin, which inhibits the COX-1 and COX-2 enzymes that produce the inflammation messenger prostaglandin, thus suppressing pain and inflammation. The poison cyanide is an irreversible enzyme inactivator that combines with the copper and iron in the active site of the enzyme cytochrome c oxidase and blocks cellular respiration.

Biological Function

Enzymes serve a wide variety of functions inside living organisms. They are indispensable for signal transduction and cell regulation, often via kinases and phosphatases. They also generate movement, with myosin hydrolysing ATP to generate muscle contraction and also moving cargo around the cell as part of the cytoskeleton. Other ATPases in the cell membrane are ion pumps involved in active transport. Enzymes are also involved in more exotic functions, such as luciferase generating light in fireflies. Viruses can also contain enzymes for infecting cells, such as the HIV integrase and reverse transcriptase, or for viral release from cells, like the influenza virus neuraminidase.

An important function of enzymes is in the digestive systems of animals. Enzymes such as amylases and proteases break down large molecules (starch or proteins, respectively) into smaller ones, so they can be absorbed by the intestines. Starch molecules, for example, are too large to be absorbed from the intestine, but enzymes hydrolyse the starch chains into smaller molecules such as maltose and eventually glucose, which can then be absorbed. Different enzymes digest different food substances. In ruminants which have a herbivorous diets, microorganisms in the gut produce another enzyme, cellulase to break down the cellulose cell walls of plant fiber

Several enzymes can work together in a specific order, creating metabolic pathways. In a metabolic pathway, one enzyme takes the product of another enzyme as a substrate. After the catalytic reaction, the product is then passed on to another enzyme. Sometimes more than one enzyme can catalyze the same reaction in parallel, this can allow more complex regulation: with for example a low constant activity being provided by one enzyme but an inducible high activity from a second enzyme.

Enzymes determine what steps occur in these pathways. Without enzymes, metabolism would neither progress through the same steps, nor be fast enough to serve the needs of the cell. Indeed, a metabolic pathway such as glycolysis could not exist independently of enzymes. Glucose, for example, can react directly with ATP to become phosphorylated at one or more of its carbons. In the absence of enzymes, this occurs so slowly as to be insignificant. However, if hexokinase is added, these slow reactions continue to take place except that phosphorylation at carbon 6 occurs so rapidly that if the mixture is tested a short time later, glucose-6-phosphate is found to be the only significant product. Consequently, the network of metabolic pathways within each cell depends on the set of functional enzymes that are present.

Control of Activity

There are five main ways that enzyme activity is controlled in the cell.

- *Enzyme production* (transcription and translation of enzyme genes) can be enhanced or diminished by a cell in response to changes in the cell's environment. This form of gene regulation is called enzyme induction and inhibition. For example, bacteria may become resistant to antibiotics such as penicillin because enzymes called beta-lactamases are induced that hydrolyse the crucial beta-lactam ring within the penicillin molecule. Another example are enzymes in the liver called cytochrome P450 oxidases, which are important in drug metabolism. Induction or inhibition of these enzymes can cause drug interactions.
- Enzymes can be *compartmentalized,* with different metabolic pathways occurring in different cellular compartments. For example, fatty acids are synthesized by one set of enzymes in the cytosol, endoplasmic reticulum and the Golgi apparatus and used by a different set of enzymes as a source of energy in the mitochondrion, through ß-oxidation.
- Enzymes can be regulated by *inhibitors and activators*. For example, the end product(s) of a metabolic pathway are often inhibitors for one of the first enzymes of the

pathway (usually the first irreversible step, called committed step), thus regulating the amount of end product made by the pathways. Such a regulatory mechanism is called a negative feedback mechanism, because the amount of the end product produced is regulated by its own concentration. Negative feedback mechanism can effectively adjust the rate of synthesis of intermediate metabolites according to the demands of the cells. This helps allocate materials and energy economically, and prevents the manufacture of excess end products. The control of enzymatic action helps to maintain a stable internal environment in living organisms.

- Enzymes can be regulated through *post-translational modification*. This can include phosphorylation, myristoylation and glycosylation. For example, in the response to insulin, the phosphorylation of multiple enzymes, including glycogen synthase, helps control the synthesis or degradation of glycogen and allows the cell to respond to changes in blood sugar. Another example of post-translational modification is the cleavage of the polypeptide chain. Chymotrypsin, a digestive protease, is produced in inactive form as chymotrypsinogen in the pancreas and transported in this form to the stomach where it is activated. This stops the enzyme from digesting the pancreas or other tissues before it enters the gut. This type of inactive precursor to an enzyme is known as a zymogen.
- Some enzymes may become *activated when localized to a different environment* (eg. from a reducing (cytoplasm) to an oxidising (periplasm) environment, high pH to low pH etc). For example, hemagglutinin in the influenza virus is activated by a conformational change caused by the acidic conditions, these occur when it is taken up inside its host cell and enters the lysosome.

Involvement in Disease

Since the tight control of enzyme activity is essential for homeostasis, any malfunction (mutation, overproduction, underproduction or deletion) of a single critical enzyme can lead to a genetic disease. The importance of enzymes is shown by the fact that a lethal illness can be caused by the malfunction of just one type of enzyme out of the thousands of types present in our bodies.

One example is the most common type of phenylketonuria. A mutation of a single amino acid in the enzyme phenylalanine hydroxylase, which catalyzes the first step in the degradation of phenylalanine, results in build-up of phenylalanine and related products. This can lead to mental retardation if the disease is untreated.

Another example is when germline mutations in genes coding for DNA repair enzymes cause hereditary cancer syndromes such as xeroderma pigmentosum. Defects in these enzymes cause cancer since the body is less able to repair mutations in the genome. This causes a slow accumulation of mutations and results in the development of many types of cancer in the sufferer.

Naming Conventions

An enzyme's name is often derived from its substrate or the chemical reaction it catalyzes, with the word ending in -ase. Examples are lactase, alcohol dehydrogenase and DNA polymerase. This may result in different enzymes, called isozymes, with the same function having the same basic name. Isoenzymes have a different amino acid sequence and might be distinguished by their optimal pH, kinetic properties or immunologically. Furthermore, the normal physiological reaction an enzyme catalyzes may not be the same as under artificial conditions. This can result in the same enzyme being identified with two different names. e.g. Glucose isomerase, used industrially to convert glucose into the sweetener fructose, is a xylose isomerase in vivo.

The International Union of Biochemistry and Molecular Biology have developed a nomenclature for enzymes, the EC numbers; each enzyme is described by a sequence of four numbers preceded by "EC". The first number broadly classifies the enzyme based on its mechanism:

The top-level classification is:

- EC 1 Oxidoreductases: catalyze oxidation/reduction reactions
- EC 2 Transferases: transfer a functional group (e.g. a methyl or phosphate group)
- EC 3 Hydrolases: catalyze the hydrolysis of various bonds
- EC 4 Lyases: cleave various bonds by means other than hydrolysis and oxidation
- EC 5 Isomerases: catalyze isomerization changes within a single molecule
- EC 6 Ligases: join two molecules with covalent bonds

Industrial Applications

Enzymes are used in the chemical industry and other industrial applications when extremely specific catalysts are required. However, enzymes in general are limited in the number of reactions they have evolved to catalyze and also by their lack of stability in organic solvents and at high temperatures. Consequently, protein engineering is an active area of research and involves attempts to create new enzymes with novel properties, either through rational design or in vitro evolution.These efforts have begun to be successful, and a few enzymes have now been desiged "from scratch" to catalyse reactions that do not occur in nature.

Enzymes are catalysts. Most are proteins. (A few ribonucleoprotein enzymes have been discovered and, for some of these, the catalytic activity is in the RNA part rather than the protein part. Link to discussion of these ribozymes.)

Enzymes bind temporarily to one or more of the reactants of the reaction they catalyze. In doing so, they lower the amount of activation energy needed and thus speed up the reaction.

Examples:

- **Catalase.** It catalyzes the decomposition of hydrogen peroxide into water and oxygen.

  $2H_2O_2 \quad 2H_2O + O_2$

  One molecule of catalase can break 40 million molecules of hydrogen peroxide each second.

- **Carbonic anhydrase.** It is found in red blood cells where it catalyzes the reaction

  $CO_2 + H_2O \quad H_2CO_3$

  It enables red blood cells to transport carbon dioxide from the tissues to the lungs.

  One molecule of carbonic anhydrase can process one million molecules of CO_2 each second.

- **Acetylcholinesterase.** It catalyzes the breakdown of the · neurotransmitter acetylcholine at several types of synapses as well as at the neuromuscular junction — the specialized synapse that triggers the contraction of skeletal muscle.

One molecule of acetylcholinesterase breaks down 25,000 molecules of acetylcholine each second. This speed makes possible the rapid "resetting" of the synapse for transmission of another nerve impulse.

Enzyme activity can be analyzed quantitatively. Some of the ways this is done are described in the page Enzyme Kinetics.

In order to do its work, an enzyme must unite — even if ever so briefly — with at least one of the reactants. In most cases, the forces that hold the enzyme and its substrate are noncovalent, an assortment of:

- hydrogen bonds
- ionic interactions
- hydrophobic interactions

Most of these interactions are weak and especially so if the atoms involved are farther than about one angstrom from each other. So successful binding of enzyme and substrate requires that the two molecules be able to approach each other closely over a fairly broad surface. Thus the analogy that a substrate molecule binds its enzyme like a key in a lock.

This requirement for complementarity in the configuration of substrate and enzyme explains the remarkable specificity of most enzymes. Generally, a given enzyme is able to catalyze only a single chemical reaction or, at most, a few reactions involving substrates sharing the same general structure.

Competitive Inhibition

The necessity for a close, if brief, fit between enzyme and substrate explains the phenomenon of competitive inhibition.

One of the enzymes needed for the release of energy within the cell is succinic dehydrogenase.

It catalyzes the oxidation (by the removal of two hydrogen atoms) of succinic acid.

(a) If one adds malonic acid to cells, or to a test tube mixture of succinic acid and the enzyme, the action of the enzyme is strongly inhibited. This is because the structure of malonic acid allows it to bind to the same site on the enzyme

(b) But there is no oxidation so no speedy release of products. The inhibition is called competitive because if you increase the ratio of succinic to malonic acid in the mixture, you will gradually restore the rate of catalysis. At a 50:1 ratio, the two molecules compete on roughly equal terms for the binding (=catalytic) site on the enzyme.

Link to a quantitative treatment of competitive inhibition.

Enzyme Cofactors

Many enzymes require the presence of an additional, nonprotein, cofactor.

- Some of these are metal ions such as Zn^{2+} (the cofactor for carbonic anhydrase), Cu^{2+}, Mn^{2+}, K^{+}, and Na^{+}.
- Some cofactors are small organic molecules called coenzymes. The B vitamins.
  - thiamine (B_1);
  - riboflavin (B_2); and
  - nicotinamide are precursors of coenzymes.

Coenzymes may be covalently bound to the protein part (called the apoenzyme) of enzymes as a prosthetic group. Others bind more loosely and, in fact, may bind only transiently to the enzyme as it performs its catalytic act.

Lysozyme: A Model of Enzyme Action

A number of lysozymes are found in nature; in human tears and egg white, for examples. The enzyme is antibacterial because it degrades the polysaccharide that is found in the cell walls of many bacteria. It does this by catalyzing the insertion of a water molecule at the position indicated by the red arrow (a glycosidic bond). This hydrolysis breaks the chain at that point.

The bacterial polysaccharide consists of long chains of alternating amino sugars:

- N-acetylglucosamine (NAG)
- N-acetylmuramic acid (NAM)

These hexose units resemble glucose except for the presence of the side chains containing amino groups.

Lysozyme is a globular protein with a deep cleft across part of its surface. Six hexoses of the substrate fit into this cleft.

- With so many oxygen atoms in sugars, as many as 14 hydrogen bonds form between the six amino sugars and certain amino acid R groups such as Arg-114, Asn-37, Asn-44, Trp-62, Trp-63, and Asp-101.
- Some hydrogen bonds also form with the C= O groups of several peptide bonds.
- In addition, hydrophobic interactions may help hold the substrate in position.

X-ray crystallography has shown that as lysozyme and its substrate unite, each is slightly deformed. The fourth hexose in the chain (ring #4) becomes twisted out of its normal position. This imposes a strain on the C-O bond on the ring-4 side of the oxygen bridge between rings 4 and 5. It is just at this J from the enzyme, and the enzyme is free to attach to a new location on the bacterial cell wall and continue its work of digesting it.

Factors Affecting Enzyme Action

The activity of enzymes is strongly affected by changes in pH and temperature. Each enzyme works best at a certain pH (left graph) and temperature (right graph), its activity decreasing at values above and below that point. This is not surprising considering the importance of:

- tertiary structure (i.e. shape) in enzyme function; and
- noncovalent forces, e.g., ionic interactions and hydrogen bonds, in determining that shape.

Examples:

- the protease pepsin works best as a pH of 1–2 (found in the stomach)

- the protease trypsin is inactive at such a low pH but very active at a pH of 8 (found in the small intestine as the bicarbonate of the pancreatic fluid neutralizes the arriving stomach contents).

Changes in pH alter the state of ionization of charged amino acids (e.g., Asp, Lys) that may play a crucial role in substrate binding and/or the catalytic action itself. Without the unionized -COOH group of Glu-35 and the ionized -COO- of Asp-52, the catalytic action of lysozyme would cease.

Hydrogen bonds are easily disrupted by increasing temperature. This, in turn, may disrupt the shape of the enzyme so that its affinity for its substrate diminishes. The ascending portion of the temperature curve (red arrow in right-hand graph above) reflects the general effect of increasing temperature on the rate of chemical reactions (graph at left). The descending portion of the curve above (blue arrow) reflects the loss of catalytic activity as the enzyme molecules become denatured at high temperatures.

Regulation of Enzyme Activity

Several mechanisms work to make enzyme activity within the cell efficient and well-coordinated.

Anchoring enzymes in membranes

Many enzymes are inserted into cell membranes, for examples:

- the plasma membrane
- the membranes of mitochondria and chloroplasts
- the endoplasmic reticulum
- the nuclear envelope

These are locked into spatial relationships that enable them to interact efficiently.

Inactive Precursors

Enzymes, such as proteases, that can attack the cell itself are inhibited while within the cell that synthesizes them. For example, pepsin is synthesized within the chief cells (in gastric glands) as an inactive precursor, pepsinogen. Only when exposed to the low pH outside the cell is the inhibiting portion of the molecule removed and active pepsin produced.

Feedback Inhibition

If the product of a series of enzymatic reactions, e.g., an amino acid, begins to accumulate within the cell, it may specifically inhibit the action of the first enzyme involved in its synthesis (red bar). Thus further production of the enzyme is hated.

Precursor Activation

The accumulation of a substance within a cell may specifically activate (blue arrow) an enzyme that sets in motion a sequence of reactions for which that substance is the initial substrate. This reduces the concentration of the initial substrate.

In the case if feedback inhibition and precursor activation, the activity of the enzyme is being regulated by a molecule which is not its substrate. In these cases, the regulator molecule binds to the enzyme at a different site than the one to which the substrate binds. When the regulator binds to its site, it alters the shape of the enzyme so that its activity is changed. This is called an allosteric effect.

- In feedback inhibition, the allosteric effect lowers the affinity of the enzyme for its substrate.
- In precursor activation, the regulator molecule increases the affinity of the enzyme in the series for its substrate.

Regulation of Enzyme Synthesis

The four mechanisms described above regulate the activity of enzymes already present within the cell.

Here, too, control mechanisms are at work that regulate the rate at which new enzymes are synthesized. Most of these controls work by turning on — or off — the transcription of genes.

If, for example, ample quantities of an amino acid are already available to the cell from its extracellular fluid, synthesis of the enzymes that would enable the cell to produce that amino acid for itself is shut down.

Conversely, if a new substrate is made available to the cell, it may induce the synthesis of the enzymes needed to cope with it. Yeast cells, for example, do not ordinarily metabolize lactose and no lactase can be detected in them. However, if grown in a medium containing lactose, they soon begin synthesizing lactase — by transcribing and translating the necessary gene(s) — and so can begin to metabolize the sugar.

CHAPTER

9

Vitamin

A vitamin is an organic compound required as a nutrient in tiny amounts by an organism A compound is called a vitamin when it cannot be synthesized in sufficient quantities by an organism, and must be obtained from the diet. Thus, the term is conditional both on the circumstances and the particular organism. For example, ascorbic acid functions as vitamin C for some animals but not others, and vitamins D and K are required in the human diet only in certain circumstances.

Vitamins are classified by their biological and chemical activity, not their structure. Thus, each "vitamin" may refer to several vitamer compounds that all show the biological activity associated with a particular vitamin. Such a set of chemicals are grouped under an alphabetized vitamin "generic descriptor" title, such as "vitamin A," which includes the compounds retinal, retinol, and many carotenoids Vitamers are often inter-converted in the body. The term vitamin does not include other essential nutrients such as dietary minerals, essential fatty acids, or essential amino acids, nor does it encompass the large number of other nutrients that promote health but are otherwise required less often.

Vitamins have diverse biochemical functions, including function as hormones (e.g. vitamin D), antioxidants (e.g. vitamin E), and mediators of cell signaling and regulators of cell and tissue growth and differentiation (e.g. vitamin A) The largest number of vitamins (e.g. B complex vitamins) function as precursors for enzyme cofactor bio-molecules (coenzymes), that help act as catalysts and substrates in metabolism. When acting as part of a catalyst, vitamins are bound to enzymes and are called prosthetic groups. For example, biotin is part of enzymes involved in making fatty acids. Vitamins also act as coenzymes to carry chemical groups between enzymes. For example, folic acid carries various forms of carbon group – methyl, formyl and methylene - in the cell. Although these roles in assisting enzyme reactions are vitamins' best-known function, the other vitamin functions are equally important.

Until the 1900s, vitamins were obtained solely through food intake, and changes in diet (which, for example, could occur during a particular growing season) can alter the types and amounts of vitamins ingested. Vitamins have been produced as commodity chemicals and made widely available as inexpensive pills for several decades,allowing supplementation of the dietary intake.

History

The Ancient Egyptians knew that feeding a patient liver (back, right) would help cure night blindness.The value of eating a certain food to maintain health was recognized long before vitamins were identified. The ancient Egyptians knew that feeding a patient liver would help cure night blindness, an illness now known to be caused by a vitamin A deficiency., however this was first discovered by Hippocrates the father of modern medicine in Ancient Greece. The advancement of ocean voyage during the Renaissance resulted in prolonged periods without access to fresh fruits and vegetables, and made illnesses from vitamin deficiency common among ship's crew.

In 1749, the Scottish surgeon James Lind discovered that citrus foods helped prevent scurvy, a particularly deadly disease in which collagen is not properly formed, causing poor wound healing, bleeding of the gums, severe pain, and death In 1753, Lind published his *Treatise on the Scurvy*, which recommended using lemons and limes to avoid scurvy, which was adopted by the British Royal Navy. This led to the nickname Limey for sailors of that organization. Lind's discovery, however, was not widely accepted by individuals in the Royal Navy's Arctic expeditions in the 19th century, where it was widely believed that scurvy could be prevented by practicing good hygiene, regular exercise, and by maintaining the morale of the crew while on board, rather than by a diet of fresh food As a result, Arctic expeditions continued to be plagued by scurvy and other deficiency diseases. In the early 20th century, when Robert Falcon Scott made his two expeditions to the Antarctic, the prevailing medical theory was that scurvy was caused by "tainted" canned food.

In 1881, Russian surgeon Nikolai Lunin studied the effects of scurvy while at the University of Tartu in present-day Estonia. He fed mice an artificial mixture of all the separate constituents of milk known at that time, namely the proteins, fats, carbohydrates, and salts. The mice that received only the individual constituents died, while the mice fed by milk itself developed normally. He made a conclusion that "a natural food such as milk must therefore contain, besides these known principal ingredients, small quantities of unknown substances essential to life. However, his conclusions were rejected by other researchers when they were unable to reproduce his results. One difference was that he had used table sugar (sucrose), while other researchers had used milk sugar (lactose) that still contained small amounts of vitamin B.

In east Asia, where polished white rice was the common staple food of the middle class, beriberi resulting from lack of vitamin B1 was endemic. In 1884, Takaki Kanehiro, a British trained medical doctor of the Japanese Navy, observed that beriberi was endemic among low-ranking crew who often ate nothing but rice, but not among crews of Western navies and officers who consumed a Western-style diet. Kanehiro initially believed that lack of protein was the chief cause of beriberi. With the support of the Japanese navy, he experimented using crews of two battleships; one crew was fed only white rice, while the other was fed a diet of meat, fish, barley, rice, and beans. The group that ate only white rice documented 161 crew members with beriberi and 25 deaths, while the latter group had only 14 cases of beriberi and no deaths. This convinced Kanehiro and the Japanese Navy that diet was the cause of beriberi. This was confirmed in 1897, when Christiaan Eijkman discovered that feeding unpolished rice instead of the polished variety to chickens helped to prevent beriberi in the chickens. The following year, Frederick Hopkins postulated that some foods contained "accessory factors"—in addition to proteins, carbohydrates, fats, et cetera—that were necessary for the functions of the human body. Hopkins was awarded the 1929 Nobel Prize for Physiology or Medicine with Christiaan Eijkman for their discovery of several vitamins.

In 1910, Japanese scientist Umetaro Suzuki succeeded in extracting a water-soluble complex of micro-nutrients from rice bran and named it 'aberic acid'. He published this discovery in a Japanese scientific journal.

When the article was translated into German, the translation failed to state that it was a newly discovered nutrient, a claim made in the original Japanese article, and hence his discovery failed to gain publicity. Polish biochemist Kazimierz Funk isolated the same complex of micronutrients and proposed the complex be named "Vitamine" (a portmanteau of "vital amine") in 1912 The name soon became synonymous with Hopkins' "accessory factors", and by the time it was shown that not all vitamins were amines, the word was already ubiquitous. In 1920, Jack Cecil Drummond proposed that the final "e" be dropped to deemphasize the "amine" reference after the discovery that vitamin C had no amine component.

Throughout the early 1900s, the use of deprivation studies allowed scientists to isolate and identify a number of vitamins. Initially, lipid from fish oil was used to cure rickets in rats, and the fat-soluble nutrient was called "antirachitic A". Thus, the first "vitamin" bioactivity ever isolated, which cured rickets, was initially called "vitamin A", although confusingly the bioactivity of this compound is now called vitamin D What we now call "vitamin A" was identified in fish oil as a separate factor that was inactivated by ultraviolet light. In 1931, Albert Szent-Györgyi and a fellow researcher Joseph Svirbely determined that "hexuronic acid" was actually vitamin C and noted its anti-scorbutic activity. In 1937, Szent-Györgyi was awarded the Nobel Prize for his discovery. In 1943 Edward Adelbert Doisy and Henrik Dam were awarded the Nobel Prize for their discovery of vitamin K and its chemical structure.

In Humans

Vitamins are classified as either water-soluble or fat soluble. In humans there are 13 vitamins: 4 fat-soluble (A, D, E and K) and 9 water-soluble (8 B vitamins and vitamin C).

Water-soluble

Water-soluble vitamins dissolve easily in water, and in general, are readily excreted from the body, to the degree that urinary output is a strong predictor of vitamin consumption. Because they are not readily stored, consistent daily intake is important Many types of water-soluble vitamins are synthesized by bacteria.

List of Vitamins

Each vitamin is typically used in multiple reactions and, therefore, most have multiple functions.

Vitamin generic descriptor name	Vitamer chemical name(s) (list not complete	Solubility	Recommended dietary allowances (male, age 19-70)	Deficiency disease	Upper Intake level (UL/day)	Overdose disease
1	2	3	4	5	6	7
Vitamin A	Retinol, retinal and four carotenoids	Fat	**900 μg**	Night-blindness and Keratomalacia	3,000 μg	Hypervitaminosis A
Vitamin B_1	Thiamine	Water	**1.2 mg**	Beriberi, Wernicke-Korsakoff syndrome	N/D	Drowsiness or muscle relaxation with large doses
Vitamin B_2	Riboflavin	Water	**1.3 mg**	Ariboflavinosis	N/D	
Vitamin B_3	Niacin, niacinamide	Water	**16.0 mg**	Pellagra	35.0 mg	Liver damage (doses>2g/day and other problems

(Contd...)

1	2	3	4	5	6	7
Vitamin B_5	Pantothenic acid	Water	5.0 mg	Paresthesia	N/D	Diarrhoea; possibly nausea and heartburn.[25]
Vitamin B_6	Pyridoxine pyriodoxamine pyridoxal	Water	**1.3–1.7 mg**	Anemia peripheral neuropathy	100 mg	Impairment of proprioception, nerve damage (doses> 100 mg/day)
Vitamin B_7	Biotin	Water	30.0 μg	Dermatitis, enteritis	N/D	
Vitamin B_9	Folic acid, folinic acid	Water	**400 μg**	Deficiency during pregnancy is associated with birth defects, such as neural tube defects	1,000 μg	May mask symptoms of vitamin B_{12} deficiency; other effects
Vitamin B_{12}	Cyanocobalamin, hydroxycobalamin, methylcobalamin	Water	**2.4 μg**	Megaloblastic anaemia[27]	N/D	No known toxicity
Vitamin C	Ascorbic acid		**90.0 mg**	Scurvy	2,000 mg	Vitamin C megadosage

(Contd…)

1	2	3	4	5	6	7
Vitamin D	Ergocalciferol, cholecalciferol	Fat	5.0 µg–10 µg	Rickets and Osteomalacia	50 µg	Hypervitaminosis D
Vitamin E	Tocopherols tocotrienols	Fat	**15.0 mg**	Deficiency is very rare; mild hemolytic anemia in newborn infants	1,000 mg	Increased congestive heart failure seen in one large randomized study
Vitamin K	Phylloquinone, menaquinones	Fat	**120 µg**	Bleeding diathesis	N/D	Increases coagulation in patients taking warfarin

Fat-soluble

Fat-soluble vitamins are absorbed through the intestinal tract with the help of lipids (fats). Because they are more likely to accumulate in the body, they are more likely to lead to hypervitaminosis than are water-soluble vitamins. Fat-soluble vitamin regulation is of particular significance in cystic fibrosis.

In Nutrition and Diseases

Vitamins are essential for the normal growth and development of a multicellular organism. Using the genetic blueprint inherited from its parents, a fetus begins to develop, at the moment of conception, from the nutrients it absorbs. It requires certain vitamins and minerals to be present at certain times. These nutrients facilitate the chemical reactions that produce among other things, skin, bone, and muscle. If there is serious deficiency in one or more of these nutrients, a child may develop a deficiency disease. Even minor deficiencies may cause permanent damage.

For the most part, vitamins are obtained with food, but a few are obtained by other means. For example, microorganisms in the intestine—commonly known as "gut flora"—produce vitamin K and biotin, while one form of vitamin D is synthesized in the skin with the help of the natural ultraviolet wavelength of sunlight. Humans can produce some vitamins from precursors they consume. Examples include vitamin A, produced from beta carotene, and niacin, from the amino acid tryptophan.

Once growth and development are completed, vitamins remain essential nutrients for the healthy maintenance of the cells, tissues, and organs that make up a multicellular organism; they also enable a multicellular life form to efficiently use chemical energy provided by food it eats, and to help process the proteins, carbohydrates, and fats required for respiration.

Deficiencies

Deficiencies of vitamins are classified as either primary or secondary. A primary deficiency occurs when an organism does not get enough of the vitamin in its food. A secondary deficiency may be due to an underlying disorder that prevents or limits the absorption or use of the vitamin, due to a "lifestyle factor", such as smoking, excessive alcohol consumption, or the use of medications that interfere with the absorption or use of the vitamin People who eat a varied diet are unlikely to develop a severe primary vitamin deficiency. In contrast, restrictive diets have the potential to cause prolonged vitamin deficits, which may result in often painful and potentially deadly diseases.

Because human bodies do not store most vitamins, humans must consume them regularly to avoid deficiency. Human bodily stores for different vitamins vary widely; vitamins A, D, and B12 are stored in significant amounts in the human body, mainly in the liver, and an adult human's diet may be deficient in vitamins A and B12 for many months before developing a deficiency condition. Vitamin B3 is not stored in the human body in significant amounts, so stores may only last a couple of weeks.

Well-known human vitamin deficiencies involve thiamine (beriberi), niacin (pellagra), vitamin C (scurvy) and vitamin D (rickets). In much of the developed world, such deficiencies are rare; this is due to:

1. an adequate supply of food; and
2. the addition of vitamins and minerals to common foods, often called fortification.

Some evidence also suggests that there is a link between vitamin deficiency and mental disorders.

Side Effects and Overdose

In large doses, some vitamins have documented side effects that tend to be more severe with a larger dosage. The likelihood of consuming too much of any vitamin from food is remote, but overdosing from vitamin supplementation does occur. At high enough dosages some vitamins cause side effects such as nausea, diarrhoea, and vomiting.

When side effects emerge, recovery is often accomplished by reducing the dosage. The concentrations of vitamins an individual can tolerate vary widely, and appear to be related to age and state of health In the United States, overdose exposure to all formulations of vitamins was reported by 62,562 individuals in 2004 (nearly 80% of these exposures were in children under the age of 6), leading to 53 "major" life-threatening outcomes and 3 deaths a small number in comparison to the 19,250 people who died of unintentional poisoning of all kinds in the U.S. in the same year (2004).

Supplements

Dietary supplements, often containing vitamins, are used to ensure that adequate amounts of nutrients are obtained on a daily basis, if optimal amounts of the nutrients cannot be obtained through a varied diet. Scientific evidence supporting the benefits of some dietary supplements is well established for certain health conditions, but others need further study. A meta-analysis in 2006 suggested that Vitamin A and E supplements not only provide no tangible health benefits for generally healthy individuals, but may actually increase mortality, although two large studies included in the analysis involved smokers, for which it was already known that beta-carotene supplements can be harmful.

In the United States, advertising for dietary supplements is required to include a disclaimer that the product is not intended to treat, diagnose, mitigate, prevent, or cure disease, and that any health claims have not been evaluated by the Food and Drug Administration In some cases, dietary supplements may have unwanted effects, especially if taken before surgery, with other dietary supplements or medicines, or if the person taking them has certain health conditions Vitamin supplements may also contain levels of vitamins many times higher, and in different forms, than one may ingest through food.

Intake of excessive quantities can cause vitamin poisoning, often due to overdose of Vitamin A and Vitamin D (The most common poisoning with multinutrient supplement pills does not involve a vitamin, but is rather due to the mineral iron). Due to toxicity, most common vitamins have recommended upper daily intake amounts.

Since 2005, suppliers have distinguished their products as either Medical Grade or Pharmaceutical Grade products. Both of these classifications indicate products that are manufactured to be easily absorbed by the body. Normal vitamin manufacturing is not regulated in the United States to the same standards as are medicinal pharmaceuticals, although U.S. vitamins which are manufactured for food consumption by humans or animals must be manufactured to Food Chemicals Codex (FCC), grade, commonly called "food grade".

Governmental Regulation of Vitamin Supplements

Most countries place dietary supplements in a special category under the general umbrella of foods, not drugs. This necessitates that the manufacturer, and not the government, be responsible for ensuring that its dietary supplement products are safe before they are marketed. Unlike drug products, which must explicitly be proven safe and effective for their intended use before marketing, there are often no provisions to "approve" dietary supplements for safety or effectiveness before they reach the consumer. Also unlike drug products, manufacturers and distributors of dietary supplements are not generally required to report any claims of injuries or illnesses that may be related to the use of their products.

Names in Current and Previous Nomenclatures

The reason the set of vitamins seems to skip directly from E to K is that the vitamins corresponding to "letters" F-J were either reclassified over time, discarded as false leads, or renamed because of their relationship to "vitamin B", which became a "complex" of vitamins. The German-speaking scientists who isolated and described vitamin K (in addition to naming it as such) did so because the vitamin is intimately involved in the Koagulation of blood following wounding. At the time, most (but not all) of the letters from F through to J were already designated, so the use of the letter K was considered quite reasonable.

Vitamins and minerals are substances that are found in foods we eat. Your body needs them to work properly, so you grow and develop just like you should. When it comes to vitamins, each one has a special role to play. For example:

- Vitamin D in milk helps your bones.
- Vitamin A in carrots helps you see at night.
- Vitamin C in oranges helps your body heal if you get a cut.
- Vitamins B in leafy green vegetables help your body make protein and energy.
- Vitamins Hang Out in Water and Fat

There are two types of vitamins: fat soluble and water soluble.

When you eat foods that contain fat-soluble vitamins, the vitamins are stored in the fat tissues in your body and in your liver. They wait around in your body fat until your body needs them.

Fat-soluble vitamins are happy to stay stored in your body for awhile — some stay for a few days, some for up to 6 months! Then, when it's time for them to be used, special carriers in your body take them to where they're needed. Vitamins A, D, E, and K are all fat-soluble vitamins.

Water-soluble vitamins are different. When you eat foods that have water-soluble vitamins, the vitamins don't get stored as much in your body. Instead, they travel through your bloodstream. Whatever your body doesn't use comes out when you urinate (pee).

So these kinds of vitamins need to be replaced often because they don't stick around! This crowd of vitamins includes vitamin C and the big group of B vitamins — B1 (thiamin), B2 (riboflavin), niacin, B6 (pyridoxine), folic acid, B12 (cobalamine), biotin, and pantothenic acid.

Vitamins Feed your Needs

Your body is one powerful machine, capable of doing all sorts of things by itself. But one thing it can't do is make vitamins. That's where food comes in. Your body is able to get the vitamins it needs from the foods you eat because different foods contain different vitamins. The key is to eat different foods to get an assortment of vitamins. Though some kids take a daily vitamin, most kids don't need one if they're eating a variety of healthy foods.

Now, let's look more closely at vitamins—from A to K:

Vitamin A

This vitamin plays a really big part in eyesight. It's great for night vision, like when you're trick-or-treating on Halloween. Vitamin A helps you see in colour, too, from the brightest yellow to the darkest purple. In addition, it helps you grow properly and aids in healthy skin. It is also a fat soluble vitamin. It can be found in fortified dairy products, fruits especially oranges and vegetables, i.e. dark green leafy vegetables (like kale, collards, spinach). Vitamin A came from animal food sources liver oils of some fish.

Vitamins B

There's more than one B vitamin. Here's the list: B_1, B_2, B_6, B_{12}, niacin, folic acid, biotin, and pantothenic acid. Whew — that's quite a group!

The B vitamins are important in metabolic (say: meh-tuh-bah-lik) activity — this means that they help make energy and set it free when your body needs it. So the next time you're running to third base, thank those B vitamins. This group of vitamins is also involved in making red blood cells, which carry oxygen throughout your body. Every part of your body needs oxygen to work properly, so these B vitamins have a really important job. Vitamin can be found in whole grains, such as wheat and oats, fish and seafood, poultry and meats, eggs, dairy products, like milk and yogurt, leafy green vegetables and beans and peas.

Vitamin C

This vitamin is important for keeping body tissues, such as gums and muscles in good shape. C is also key if you get a cut or wound because it helps you heal. This vitamin also helps your body resist infection. This means that even though you can't always avoid getting sick, vitamin C makes it a little harder for your body to become infected with an illness.

Best sources are citrus fruits, like oranges, cantaloupe , strawberries, tomatoes, broccoli, cabbage, kiwi fruit, sweet red peppers, kiwi, grapes etc.

Vitamin D

No bones about it ... vitamin D is the vitamin you need for strong bones! It's also great for forming strong teeth. Vitamin D even lends a hand to an important mineral — it helps your body absorb the amount of calcium it needs. Vitamin D is present in milk fortified with vitamin D, fish, egg yolks, liver, fortified cereal, cod liver oil, fortified cereals, cream and so on.

Vitamin E

Everybody needs vitamin E. This hard-working vitamin maintains a lot of your body's tissues, like the ones in your eyes, skin, and liver. It protects your lungs from becoming damaged by polluted air, and it is important for the formation of red blood cells. It has strong antioxidant properties. This vitamin protect against heart disease and cancer. It is found in whole grains, such as wheat and oats, wheat germ, leafy green vegetables, sardines, egg yolks, nuts and seeds, sunflower, safflower etc.

Vitamin K

Vitamin K is the clotmaster! Remember the last time you got a cut? Your blood did something special called clotting. This is when certain cells in your blood act like glue and stick together at the surface of the cut to help stop the bleeding. Vitamin K is found in leafy green vegetables, dairy products, like milk and yogurt, broccoli, soybean oil etc.

CHAPTER

10

Food Additive

Food additives are substances added to food to preserve flavour or improve its taste and appearance. Some additives have been used for centuries; for example, preserving food by pickling (with vinegar), salting, as with bacon, preserving sweets or using sulfur dioxide as in some wines. With the advent of processed foods in the second half of the 20th century, many more additives have been introduced, of both natural and artificial origin.

Numbering

To regulate these additives, and inform consumers, each additive is assigned a unique number. Initially these were the "E numbers" used in Europe for all approved additives. This numbering scheme has now been adopted and extended by the Codex Alimentarius Commission to internationally identify all additives, regardless of whether they are approved for use.

E numbers are all prefixed by "E", but countries outside Europe use only the number, whether the additive is approved in Europe or not. For example, acetic acid is written as E260 on products sold in Europe, but is simply known as additive 260 in some countries. Additive 103, alkanet, is not approved for use in Europe so does not have an E number, although it is approved for use in Australia and New Zealand. Since 1987 Australia has had an approved system of labelling for additives in packaged foods. Each food additive has to be named or numbered. The numbers are the same as in Europe, but without the prefix 'E'.

The United States Food and Drug Administration listed these items as "Generally recognized as safe" or GRAS and these are listed under both their Chemical Abstract Services number and FDA regulation listed under the US Code of Federal Regulations.

Acids

Food acids are added to make flavors "sharper", and also act as preservatives and antioxidants. Common food acids include vinegar, citric acid, tartaric acid, malic acid, fumaric acid, lactic acid.

Acidity Regulators

Acidity regulators are used to change or otherwise control the acidity and alkalinity of foods.

Anticaking Agents

Anticaking agents keep powders such as milk powder from caking or sticking.

Antifoaming Agents

Antifoaming agents reduce or prevent foaming in foods.

Antioxidants

Antioxidants such as vitamin C act as preservatives by inhibiting the effects of oxygen on food, and can be beneficial to health.

Bulking Agents

Bulking agents such as starch are additives that increase the bulk of a food without affecting its nutritional value.

Food Colouring

Colorings are added to food to replace colors lost during preparation, or to make food look more attractive.

Colour Retention Agents

In contrast to colourings, color retention agents are used to preserve a food's existing colour.

Emulsifiers

Emulsifiers allow water and oils to remain mixed together in an emulsion, as in mayonnaise, ice cream, and homogenized milk.

Flavours

Flavours are additives that give food a particular taste or smell, and may be derived from natural ingredients or created artificially.

Flavour Enhancers

Flavour enhancers enhance a food's existing flavors. They may be extracted from natural sources (through distillation, solvent extraction, maceration, among other methods) or created artificially.

Flour Treatment Agents

Flour treatment agents are added to flour to improve its color or its use in baking.

Humectants

Humectants prevent foods from drying out.

Tracer Gas

Tracer gas allow for package integrity testing to prevent foods from being exposed to atmosphere, thus guaranteeing shelf life.

Preservatives

Preservatives prevent or inhibit spoilage of food due to fungi, bacteria and other microorganisms.

Stabilizers

Stabilizers, thickeners and gelling agents, like agar or pectin (used in jam for example) give foods a firmer texture. While they are not true emulsifiers, they help to stabilize emulsions.

Sweeteners

Sweeteners are added to foods for flavoring. Sweeteners other than sugar are added to keep the food energy (calories) low, or because they have beneficial effects for diabetes mellitus and tooth decay and diarrhea.

Thickeners

Thickeners are substances which, when added to the mixture, increase its viscosity without substantially modifying its other properties.

Safety

With the increasing use of processed foods since the 19th century, there has been a great increase in the use of food additives of varying levels of safety. This has led to legislation in many countries regulating their use. For example, boric acid was widely used as a food preservative from the 1870s to the 1920s but was banned after World War I due to its toxicity, as demonstrated in animal and human studies. During World War II the urgent need for cheap, available food preservatives led to it being used again, but it was finally banned in the 1950s Such cases led to a general mistrust of food additives, and an application of the precautionary principle led to the conclusion that only additives that are known to be safe should be used in foods. In the USA, this led to the adoption of the Delaney clause, an amendment to the Federal Food, Drug, and Cosmetic Act of 1938, stating that no carcinogenic substances may be used as food additives. However, after the banning of cyclamates in the USA and Britain in 1969, saccharin, the only remaining legal artificial sweetener at the time, was found to cause cancer in rats. Widespread public outcry in the USA, partly communicated to Congress by postage-paid postcards supplied in the packaging of sweetened soft drinks, led to the retention of saccharin despite its violation of the Delaney clause.

Cases like these serve to highlight the controversy associated with the risks and benefits of food additives. Some artificial food additives have been linked with cancer, digestive problems, and neurological conditions such as ADD, or diseases like heart disease or obesity Even "natural" additives may be harmful, whether because of overuse (for example table salt) or because of natural toxicity. An example is safrole, which was used to flavour root beer until it was shown to be carcinogenic. Due to the application of the Delaney clause, it may not be added to foods, even though it occurs naturally in sassafras and sweet basil.

LIST OF FOOD ADDITIVES

- Acidity regulators;
- Anti-caking agents;
- Anti-foaming agents;
- Food colouring;
- Colour fixatives;
- Colour retention agents;
- Emulsifiers;

- Firming agents;
- Flavours enhancer;
- Flour treatment agents;
- Food acids;
- Gelling agents;
- Glazing agents;
- Humectants;
- Improving agents;
- Mineral salts;
- Preservatives;
- Antioxidants;
- Propellants;
- Seasonings;
- Sequestrants;
- Stabilizers;
- Sweeteners;
  Artificial sweeteners;
- Thickeners;
- Vegetable gums.

Caffeine and other GRAS (generally recognized as safe) additives such as sugar and salt are not required to go through the regulation process.

Index

X

❑❑❑